Christopher Lowell

BBC MUSIC GUIDES

———

ELGAR ORCHESTRAL MUSIC

£3—

PA

BBC MUSIC GUIDES

General editor: GERALD ABRAHAM

Bach Cantatas J. A. WESTRUP

Beethoven Piano Sonatas DENIS MATTHEWS

Beethoven Symphonies ROBERT SIMPSON

Berlioz Orchestral Music HUGH MACDONALD

Brahms Orchestral Music JOHN HORTON

Debussy Piano Music FRANK DAWES

Haydn String Quartets ROSEMARY HUGHES

Haydn Symphonies H. C. ROBBINS LANDON

Monteverdi Madrigals DENIS ARNOLD

Mozart Chamber Music A. HYATT KING

Ravel Orchestral Music LAURENCE DAVIES

Schubert Chamber Music J. A. WESTRUP

Schubert Piano Sonatas PHILIP RADCLIFFE

Schubert Songs MAURICE J. E. BROWN

Schubert Symphonies MAURICE J. E. BROWN

Tchaikovsky Symphonies and Concertos JOHN WARRACK

BBC MUSIC GUIDES

Elgar Orchestral Music

MICHAEL KENNEDY

BRITISH BROADCASTING CORPORATION

In Memoriam R.H.W.

Contents

Introduction	5	*Falstaff*	32
Style and Method	8	*Pomp and Circumstance*	35
'Songs of Innocence'	17	*Serenade*	39
Variations on an Original		*Introduction and Allegro*	40
Theme (Enigma)	21	Violin Concerto	43
Froissart	28	Cello Concerto	46
Cockaigne	29	Symphony No. 1	53
In the South	30	Symphony No. 2	57

Music example no. 15 is reproduced by permission of Boosey and Hawkes (Music Publishers) Ltd, and no. 17 by British and Continental Music Agencies Ltd. All the remaining examples are by permission of Novello & Co. Ltd.

Published by the British Broadcasting Corporation
35 Marylebone High Street, London W1M 4AA

SBN 563 10150 4
First published 1970
© Michael Kennedy 1970

Printed in England by
Cox & Wyman Ltd, London, Reading and Fakenham

Introduction

Elgar's mastery of the orchestra has never been disputed; even when his music was 'out of fashion' towards the end of his life his detractors invariably conceded that he ranked among the great orchestrators. What remains remarkable, even miraculous, is that this mastery was self-taught, by precept and practice. Born in 1857 near Worcester, where his father owned a music-shop, tuned pianofortes, played the organ at church, sold sheet-music and taught, Edward Elgar grew up among music and musical instruments. As a very small boy he was discovered down by the River Severn 'trying to write down what the reeds were saying'; later in life he told an acquaintance that he had always had 'musical day-dreams in the same way that other people had day-dreams of heroism and adventure; he could express almost any thought that came into his head in terms of music'. Whereas this precocious flair for music might in better-off households have led to some kind of academic instruction or even to entry into one of the foreign conservatoires, such as Leipzig, no such course was possible for Elgar, the fourth of seven children of a father whose head for business was casual to say the least. Although Elgar seems never to have forgiven 'providence' for his lowly birth and the struggles it entailed, at least he did not have to overcome the prevalent English mid-Victorian middle-class prejudice against the arts, and especially music, as a profession, or even sometimes as an all-absorbing hobby. His parents loved music and literature and took it for granted that their children would want to play instruments and study scores; the Three Choirs Festival was a major feature of the background of his adolescence; local choral societies and orchestras formed a permanent part of the pattern of life. So if Edward wanted to study a Mozart, Handel or Beethoven score, there it was in the shop, to hand. So were books on counterpoint, harmony, composition and orchestration. We can imagine him, like the boy in Whitman's *Sea-Drift*, 'peering, absorbing, translating'.

This was the theoretical side of his self-education. Even more important was the practical. When very young, Elgar could play the organ and the pianoforte but the instrument he loved was the violin. He played in most of the Worcester amateur orchestras and eventually among the first violins of the orchestra at the Three Choirs Festival. When he was twenty he saved the money to go to London for lessons from Adolphe Pollitzer but abandoned them when he realised that he had not a sufficiently big tone to become a front-rank virtuoso. Thenceforward he was content to remain an orchestral player; and by now, too, he was in demand as a conductor, often called upon to 'arrange' music by Wagner or Beethoven for a small combination of instruments and sometimes to provide something of his own. Undoubtedly the most valuable experience for him came in 1879 when he was appointed conductor of the band at Worcester City and County Pauper Lunatic Asylum, Powick, which gave concerts for the entertainment of the staff. He had played in the band since 1877; at the same time he was also a member of a wind quintet (bassoon, played by Elgar, two flutes, oboe, clarinet). For the asylum band and for the quintet he wrote and arranged music, and in doing so he learned the capabilities, needs and quirks of individual instruments so that he never wrote an impossible or distorted part for any instrument in any of his works. The asylum staff apparently enjoyed dancing quadrilles, of which he wrote many. One, the fifth of a set of five called *L'Assommoir*, was pressed into service again thirty years later as 'The Wild Bears' in the second *Wand of Youth* suite:

Ex. 1

The answer, then, to the question 'How did Elgar, born in a provincial cathedral city, become without any academic tuition an orchestrator the equal of Berlioz and Tchaikovsky?' is: by reading, by studying other men's scores, by writing music for amateur combinations of instruments, by conducting, by teaching, by playing and also (for he worked in the shop, it must be remembered) by repairing instruments and by selling them. Also, of course, by something else. As Toscanini said, 'All you need, to be a composer, is a little genius.'

Genius is not a word to use lightly; and it is certainly a word to use precisely. 'Extraordinary capacity for imaginative creation', the dictionary says; and in considering Elgar's music it is the imaginative quality that must constantly be in the forefront of our minds. No survey of his orchestral output can deal exclusively with the notes and harmonies as written in the scores. Although by technical analysis one can isolate the virus in any particular passage, and although the music itself is strong enough to be self-sufficient examined and heard purely as a musical structure, yet by excluding extra-musical clues and associations, whether personal or literary, a dimension is eradicated. In Elgar's case, more than in many another composer's, the music is such a personal expression that his clues to its 'meaning', even in non-programmatic works, are a valuable adjunct to understanding and not, as so often happens, a red herring or deliberately misleading.

And how vividly he did express himself, with all the candour of a Rembrandt self-portrait, in his music. The sharp divisions in his psychological make-up are all delineated in his orchestral works: the exuberance and joviality, the black despair, the assertiveness, the dreams by the riverside. Somewhere at the heart of all the works is the lonely, discontented man whose gift for friendship and whose hard-won fame never really overcame the defect in his personality which could lead him to excuse himself at the last moment from a dinner-party because, as he told his hostess, 'You will not wish your table to be disgraced by the son of a piano-tuner.' That was said in 1897, when his rise to eminence was only beginning. When he had composed two masterpieces, the *Enigma Variations* and *The Dream of Gerontius*, he could still say, 'Just like my influence on everything and everybody – always evil!' And at the very end of his life, when he was baronet, Master of the King's Musick, O.M., the unchallenged personification of English music, he pathetically wrote to the boy Menuhin's father asking him to consider 'if it will not be a risk for Yehudi's immense fame and position to be associated with me'.

He was truly a Romantic, relating his art to life, to his own feelings on every subject. He admitted it: 'I was dreaming of . . . some lovely remembrance of long ago idylls . . . well, I have put it all in my music, and also much more that has never happened.' He put it all in, whether it was a dream of what might have been, an idealisation of a woman, or his delight in Falstaff falling into a drunken sleep or his friend's dog swimming in the Wye. That is what is meant by Elgarian.

Style and Method

Sir Neville Cardus, in a memorable essay on Elgar in his *A Composers' Eleven*,* wrote: 'He pointed no new direction. If he had never composed a note, there would today be no link missing from the main evolution of the vocabulary and syntax of music.' Much the same could, of course, be said of Brahms: there is no reason why a composer should be a pioneer. But Elgar's use of the 'language of music', as he found it, is oft-times so original and inventive that it seems as if he ventured along new paths, though none followed him there because his style and methods are so personal. It is worth spending a little time examining those methods, for which the adjective 'Elgarian' is sufficient description to bring them clearly to mind.

First, which composers influenced him (because no composer is entirely uninfluenced by others)? We know that he had no use for the early English composers, with the exception of some Purcell, who, in one of his Birmingham lectures, he called 'our greatest'. Byrd, Weelkes, Tallis and Dowland were 'museum pieces' as far as Elgar was concerned. But Handel was a different matter. When Herbert Howells asked him the secret of the power and resonance of his writing for strings, Elgar replied: 'You'll find the answer in Handel – I went to him for help ages ago.' I suspect that it was the concerti grossi to which he went, for in them can plainly be heard the ingredients of Elgar's 'noble' style as well as of the restrained sweetness with which it is so often contrasted. 'Schumann – my ideal', he wrote in 1883, and there are Elgarian

* Collins, 1958.

pre-echoes in the D minor Symphony and the *Manfred* music. Dvořák, too, he admired greatly and he seems to have learned much from him about the use of flecks of woodwind tone to emphasise the salient features of a phrase. The influence of Brahms is more apparent in the chamber music, especially the Piano Quintet, than in the orchestral works, but Brahms's Third Symphony, which Elgar admired with some reservations and conducted, and about which he gave a most perceptive lecture in 1905, is Elgarian in its enigmatic mood (hence its appeal to him, perhaps) and has the close thematic relationships that are the distinguishing feature of Elgar's treatment of symphonic form. Also there is a suggestion of flattery by imitation on Elgar's part in the finale of his First Symphony where the second subject of the finale

Ex. 2

behaves in an identical manner to its exact counterpart in the finale of Brahms's symphony. Both have a bass moving in crotchets beneath a theme in triplets on cellos, repeated an octave higher by the first violins.

Elgar's chromaticism, the sign-manual of the late romantic, obviously owes much to the example of Wagner. As Arthur Johnstone wrote in 1900, 'it is not allowable for a modern composer of religious music to be ignorant of *Parsifal*', and in *Gerontius* there are recollections of Amfortas. But Elgar's methods are not Wagner's, and if many of his harmonic progressions are Wagnerian in origin they sound Elgarian in performance. Even less obvious is the influence of his contemporary Richard Strauss – the 'greatest living composer' in Elgar's 1905 opinion – for only the very beginning of *In the South*, an unconscious echo perhaps of *Don Juan*, is in any way Straussian, with divided strings and brass bestriding them heroically. *Falstaff*'s final pages are sometimes compared with those of *Don Quixote*, but not by anybody who knows the two works. If there is Straussian influence in *Falstaff*, it can, I suggest, be found in the Gadshill episode where Act III of *Der Rosenkavalier* – the discomfiture of Ochs – is a possible model. In any case Strauss and Elgar inhabited different worlds of emotion, Elgar being in every respect a more 'spiritual' composer than the fleshy, worldly Strauss.

Elgar was contemptuous of folk-music and his occasional modality is probably derived from church music. That he studied the scores of Verdi, notably of *Aïda*, seems obvious from his scoring for brass. But whence came that admirable clarity which distinguishes all his orchestral music so that Tovey, for instance, wished that 'many an ambitious composer of brilliant and revolutionary reputation' could be 'washed' in the crystal-clear scoring of the *Enigma Variations*? The answer, in my opinion, is from the late-nineteenth-century French composers whose music Elgar knew well and conducted at Worcester – from Massenet, Saint-Saëns and especially from Delibes, whom he greatly admired. From them, and from Dvořák, he learned economy and the value of contrasts of dynamics and instrumentation. Elgar's scores are rightly called opulent as far as tone-colour is concerned, but they are never congested. In his absorbing lecture on orchestration* Elgar showed himself fully aware of the dangers inherent in mishandling the modern symphony orchestra ('the mighty engine, the vehicle of the highest form of art ever known to the world'). He said: 'The tendency of the moment is to use this great machine too continuously at something approaching the full power. . . . If the composer finds he has written at all simply, he seems to be possessed with a nervous feeling that "something is wrong".' Elgar almost always wrote 'simply', in that he compels his orchestra to give a forthright, direct account of his meaning as expressed in instrumental terms.

Elgar's orchestration is firmly based on the strings: they are the ocean on which the other instruments glide or toss. When they surge like a groundswell, the rest of the orchestra is often in ferment; when they provide a calm surface, other instruments glint and shine, just as yachts with coloured sails decorate the

* Reprinted in *A Future for English Music and other Lectures* (ed. Percy M. Young) (Dobson, 1968).

sea with their colour and graceful movement. Elgar never writes harshly for the strings: a rich, mellow sound is characteristic, quite unmistakable in its ability to project an emotional quality which Elgar himself described as 'smiling with a sigh'. This quality is achieved by use of plagal cadences, as in the second interlude in *Falstaff*, where the tonality is also indeterminate, and in 'The Wagon Passes' in the *Nursery Suite* where again minor intervals create the effect of wistful regret. A notable moment occurs in the third movement (*adagio*) of the First Symphony when the second subject is played by the violins, then by cellos and basses over which violins, with the harps, play triplets which give an effect of flight. No wonder that Samuel Langford, in another context, wrote of the music 'inhabiting the air' and 'the music's wings' in connection with Elgar. Solos for the string instruments provide memorable episodes in many of his works: the viola's misty entry in the Prelude to *Gerontius*, for example, and in the 'Dorabella' variation, the viola solo when the 'Welsh tune' is first introduced in the *Introduction and Allegro* for strings

Ex. 3

and, perhaps most beautiful of all, the viola solo in the *canto popolare* section of *In the South* (see Ex. 13).

The solo violin is used almost vocally on several occasions, the greatest perhaps being in *Falstaff*, where in the first interlude it represents Falstaff's (i.e. Elgar's) dream of the lost days of his youth, and in the 'Envoy' of the *Nursery Suite* where a similar mood is captured and in addition one senses the old composer looking back to his youthful hopes of being a violin virtuoso, introducing the reminiscences of earlier themes like a storyteller. Clarinet solos abound, his use of this instrument being especially happy and sensitive. (What a clarinet quintet he might have written!) One has only to recall the two notes perfectly placed at the end of the *adagio* of the First Symphony, the Mendelssohn quotation in the 'Romanza' Variation, several examples in *The Wand of Youth*, and the little fragments of phrases that bestrew the second movement of the Cello Concerto. The long, semi-improvisatory oboe solo which trails a melancholy counterpoint above divided violins, violas and cellos and the pizzicato tread of the basses in the *larghetto* of the Second Symphony is one of Elgar's most inspired pieces of orchestration, and he uses the oboe more briefly but equally poignantly in *Gerontius* at the words 'manhood crucified'.

His use of brass is invariably skilful; he can have it aptly strident as in *Cockaigne* and the finale of the *Variations* or gorgeously mellow as in the slow movements of the symphonies. In both symphonies there are passages when a trumpet pierces the texture of the score over an excited accompaniment, a moment of high drama in each case, like an actor's sudden entry on the stage. Horns are used as blending instruments, often taking the strings through a harmonic change. Trombones are reserved for solemn moments and are blended surprisingly but perfectly with the solo violin in the Violin Concerto's second movement. Like all romantic composers, Elgar makes effective use of the harp when he wants the texture to glisten, as in the last pages of the Second Symphony and in the 'river music' of the second movement of the First Symphony; and percussion, too, are called upon many times for poetic or crucial effects, instances being the timpani roll played with two coins to represent the liner's engines in the 'Romanza' Variation, the little outburst for side-drum in *Falstaff* and the final shrill drum-roll in the same work.

Elgar used a large orchestra but he rarely indulged in exotic instrumental forces, and then only for particular effects – the tabor in the orchard scene in *Falstaff*, and the straight trumpet for the shofar in *The Apostles*. He asks for the organ in *Cockaigne* and the *Variations*, the glockenspiel in *In the South,* the bass clarinet often and an E flat clarinet in the Second Symphony. Surprisingly he confessed to having wanted four saxophones in *Caractacus* but the difficulty in finding players and the expense of rehearsing forced him to abandon the idea: he considered that the instrument was 'beautiful and expressive and, if you wish, subdued'. He never wrote for it in any of his later works.

A feature of Elgar's scoring, of which the trumpet highlights mentioned above are exemplary, is his invariable coinciding of the climax of the music with a climax of tone. The *Variations* are full of examples of an instrument being used to double perhaps no more than half a dozen notes at a climacteric: oboe with the cellos and violas in 'B.G.N.', oboe and clarinet with strings in 'Nimrod', also oboe and strings in 'Fairy Pipers' (*Wand of Youth*). Trombones point up the pizzicato strings in *Cockaigne*, flecks of woodwind add brightness to many a string passage in the First Symphony, and there is a superb passage in *In the South* where the cor anglais gives rhythmic as well as melodic aid to the theme in the lower strings, horns and clarinets. It is by devices such as this, coupled with detailed instructions on bowing and dynamics, that Elgar ensures that the orchestra phrases the music as he wishes. He leaves nothing to chance, yet he leaves the conductor latitude for 'interpretation'.

What gives Elgar's tunes their personal quality and family relationship? Primarily his predilection for the interval of the seventh and the sixth, one rising and one dropping. He liked phrases which leap upward – 'Leap, leap to the light' (*Caractacus*) might be taken as the motto for these tunes – and themes which derived from a simple rhythmical pattern, a typical example being the main theme of the last movement of the Second Symphony. His use of sequences has often been commented upon, generally adversely, and it is true that there are occasions (the finale of the Second Symphony again being a case in point) when he seems to be using sequences as a platoon sergeant might use the command 'Mark time' while he works out what on earth to do next. But when he uses them for modulation – something that Bruckner never learned to do – at intervals of a third, and especially when (as in the Violin Concerto) they are irregular or 'out of step', the effect is magnificent and unmistakable. So too is the method by which he obtains the effects both of restlessness and of nervous energy – the constant switching of tonality, often to remote keys. In fact it is often extremely difficult to decide the tonality of particular passages, and it is just this ambiguity which gives the music its incomparable effect of being wide-spanned or, as Cardus poetically put it, of opening 'our enchanted ears upon new faery seas of tone'.

Of more interest and importance to the general listener is

Elgar's method of symphonic construction and composition. There is no doubt that he relied more on texture than on structure to carry the main force of his thought, but the once widely-propagated criticism that Elgar's symphonies were sprawling, formless rhapsodies, colourful rather than cogent, was scotched once and for all by Diana McVeagh in her splendid book on Elgar.* The composer himself, always articulate, provided the important clues through two nouns that he applied to himself – incubator and oven. Themes 'incubated' for years, as a study of his sketchbooks shows. There are dozens of examples of his putting to use themes or quite large sections of music twenty years after they were composed, like Beethoven. He told Sanford Terry that the climax of a movement and its general shape occurred to him first, and that associated with these was 'a great mass of fluctuating material which *might* fit into the work as it developed in his mind'. This material Elgar often wrote out in short score as a musical paragraph, and we have W. H. Reed's evidence of Elgar pinning up bits of the Violin Concerto ready for him to play.

If this seems haphazard and illogical – and Elgar once told his friend A. J. Jaeger, 'You won't frighten me into writing a logically developed movement where I don't want one' – it has to be remembered that the material all came 'from the same oven', in other words the relationship of one theme to another is extraordinarily and intricately close. His symphonic method is not classical but is more akin to that of Sibelius – or Mahler. All three composers are concerned with the germination of cells of theme rather than with exposition and development in the Viennese style. Elgar is constantly showing how one theme is related to another; in both symphonies and in the Violin Concerto he is concerned to show the common stem of all the themes. Some of the connections are subtle, for example the opening bars of the Second Symphony (see Ex. 28) and the first theme of its slow movement:

Ex. 4

* *Edward Elgar: his life and music* (Dent, 1955).

The opening themes of the first and second movements of the Violin Concerto are from the same oven

Ex. 5
Allegro

Ex. 6
Andante

and the cadenza of this great work brings into close-up the common features of all its main themes. Then there are the reintroduction of a theme from the first movement of the Second Symphony into the rondo to precipitate the remarkable outburst of frenzy, and the transformation of the theme of the second movement of the First Symphony into the *adagio* theme (Ex. 27). The *adagio* of the First Symphony provides a major example of Elgar's composition of the climax first: the sketch for the wonderful *molto espressivo* theme at cue 104 is dated 21 August 1904, three years before most of the work was written. Yet the movement sounds as logical and fluent as if it had been composed in exact sequence. Many of the thematic relationships are achieved by a use of counterpoint so masterly that it amounts to sleight of hand.

Elgar's mind was both complex and clear. He loved puzzles and codes and acrostics, and it is not surprising therefore that his development sections are in effect a tangle – an organised tangle – of cross-references, allusions, a detail spotlighted here and there and shown to be a fiery particle of a main theme. Since he was astute in ferreting out similar allusions in other men's music, it is reasonable to assume that most of his own were conscious, not subconscious. Yet he said 'I feel, I don't invent', and his manuscripts show how often he had a brilliant afterthought, as if he had suddenly perceived another resemblance and had found a poetical way of establishing it. Also, there is the evidence of his letter to Jaeger in which he says that he did not notice till long after the score had been engraved that Gerontius's 'in thine own agony' and the chords introducing the Angel of the Agony were akin, 'but they are, aren't they?' Contemplating Elgar's system of composing brings to mind the parts of a watch, scattered on a table in a seemingly unrelated muddle. Yet, assembled by the watchmaker, in whose mind is the key to the relationship of each part, the watch becomes not only an ordered mechanism but goes, too. It is Elgar's secret how he managed to impart an air of spontaneity to this intricate process, a process that establishes him as one of the outstanding intellects of music, cool-headed and clear-brained to achieve results in which the blood courses hotly as though from unconsidered impulse. No wonder he said of any passage that he felt was specially alive, 'If you cut that it would bleed!'

There remains for discussion here, before individual works are examined, the paradox that, whereas Elgar's music was first appreciated at its true worth by continental musicians – Richter, Brodsky, Kreisler, Steinbach, Buths, Strauss, Backhaus, Weingartner – who perceived that it was in the European tradition, nevertheless it is for very many people the quintessence of Englishness. (Eric Fenby, for instance, says that he became homesick when he heard Elgar's music, not Delius's.) One explanation may be that, for all his overt romanticism, for all the so-called opulence, he is usually reticent in his emotional expression. The music is impassioned and the man was passionate, but the music is never sensuous. There is nothing in Elgar like the 'Hero's Love' in *Ein Heldenleben* or the love scene from Berlioz's *Romeo and Juliet*. A foreign commentator, Adolfo Salazar, found Elgar 'cold and courtly' and even Samuel Langford, as late as 1924, wrote of his music as 'cold' and 'rich in English hardness'. The emotional basis of Elgar's music is often concerned with moral and spiritual qualities or picturesque detail: the ideal of friendship in the *Variations*, the idealisation of love in the Violin Concerto, the yearning for a land of lost content in the Second Symphony and the *Wand of Youth*. The First Symphony, he said, was concerned with 'a great charity (love) and a *massive* hope for the future'. We are forced back, however reluctantly, to Elgar's much-quoted remark about music being 'in the air all around us'. No technical analysis can discover for certain just how he took something from

16

the air of the Malvern Hills, from the banks of the Teme and Severn, from the cloisters of Worcester Cathedral, and turned it into music which speaks immediately and directly of these things to his fellow-countrymen. Walk in Worcestershire and the music of Elgar is in the air around you, fantastic as this may seem to the prosaically minded. Genius has the right to retain its mysteries and its magic. But there is a penalty to be paid, and if Elgar's music, despite its superb orchestration, has not won the affection of conductors of all nationalities as Brahms's has, it is because of its elusive emotional nature, which requires special sympathies and experience. In one sense the music 'plays itself'; but notwithstanding all the detailed marks of expression, Elgar needs something a good deal better and subtler than just a 'straightforward account of the score'.

'Songs of Innocence'

Elgar was an orchestral composer before all else. His earliest sketches were instrumental and in his adolescence it was chamber music or music for orchestral forces that contained the strongest hints of the master-to-be. His songs and church music were much inferior and convey the impression of having been written as an exercise or from a sense of duty. The first work of his performed by Stockley's orchestra in Birmingham in 1883 was a *Sérénade mauresque* and the first Elgar work played in London, in 1884, was another orchestral piece, *Sevillana*. Both were praised for their scoring. The *Sérénade mauresque* was incorporated into a Suite in D of four movements, which Stockley conducted in 1888, and August Manns at the Crystal Palace a little later. In 1899 Elgar revised the suite, dropped one movement (a march) and retitled it *Three Characteristic Pieces,* Op. 10. Scored for small orchestra, they have a distinctive charm, especially No. 3, 'The Gavotte, A.D. 1700 and 1900', a piece of gentle pastiche in which the 'Enigma' theme is faintly foreshadowed:

Ex. 7

The interesting point about Elgar's juvenilia is that they show how early his distinctive tone of voice was audible – which is only one way of saying that his style was natural to him, born in him. It could hardly have been otherwise, for there was no one to teach him or to persuade him to model himself on some other favoured composer, for which we must be very thankful. He kept all his early pieces and ransacked them throughout his life when he wanted a tune or an idea. That is why it is always dangerously misleading to say when any particular piece by Elgar was composed; its publication and performance dates might be years later. Sketchbooks dated 1879, when he was at Powick, contain the *Sérénade mauresque* and many sections of the *Wand of Youth* music, although these were probably rewritten versions, for the play itself was performed about ten years earlier. A hymn he wrote in 1878 was used in the *Nursery Suite* (1931). The Powick quadrilles yielded several later transformations.

These early manifestations are not only important historically. They demonstrate that Elgar was always wholly himself. If this seems obvious, it is because our understanding of Elgar is today so much more perceptive than it was in the 1920–40 era. Then it was axiomatic that criticism divided him down the centre: on one side the composer of light pieces, salon music, pot-boilers, beneath the notice of those who gave the cosmos its A (and also, come to that, of the coiner of that phrase, Ernest Newman); on the other, the great composer of the major works. To these people it was incomprehensible how Elgar suddenly produced the *Variations* in 1899, perpetually puzzling that the two bodies of work should have flowed from the same pen. But in 1970 the unity between the salon pieces, the childhood suites, the marches and the large-scale works is clearly apparent. In both we find the sudden contrasts of extrovert gaiety and dark despair, of almost physical exuberance and sudden still melancholy. No one today is likely to put his nose in the air at *Salut d'amour* if it is heard in the original orchestration. More characteristically Elgarian, however, are the *Chanson de nuit* and *Chanson de matin*, Op. 15, nos. 1 and 2, published in 1897 in their original versions for violin and pianoforte and in the orchestral versions which are usually heard today. Almost certainly they were written nearly ten years earlier.

A major emotional factor in Elgar's music is his nostalgia for the days of his childhood. Perhaps he looked at them through rose-coloured spectacles, because he maintained in his maturity that 'no one was ever kind' to him then, and *The Wand of Youth* itself was a play devised by the Elgar children in a rebellious mood – it was about a perfect world, remarkably anticipating Barrie, from which grumpy adults were barred and only children, moths and butterflies, wild and tame bears, and fairies and giants admitted. Wistful stillnesses occur in the symphonies and concertos, in *Falstaff* and in smaller pieces, when Elgar is obviously once again, as he put it at the age of 64, 'the dreamy child who used to be found in the reeds by Severn side . . . longing for something very great'. In the two *Wand of Youth* Suites, the *Severn Suite*, the *Nursery Suite*, and in some slighter pieces, Elgar deliberately re-captured this boyhood mood. They are his 'songs of innocence'.

It is not clear just when the Elgar children performed their play, *The Wand of Youth,* or where. They had left the cottage at Broad-heath, where Elgar was born, in 1859, but returned to stay at a farm near by. The first theme of 'Fairies and Giants' is scribbled in one of Elgar's sketchbooks as 'Humoresque Broadheath, 1867'. He himself also gave 1869 and 1871 as conflicting dates of the play; anyway, he was about twelve when he wrote the music. In the stage directions there is a 'woodland glade, intersected by a brook' (the children's exclusive world was on the other side of the brook) and this may have been a reference to the cottage garden.

Elgar composed – or, to be accurate, revised and rescored – the music of *The Wand of Youth* Suites in the spring of 1907, before he began serious work on the First Symphony. 'Poor things but mine own boyish thoughts', he modestly called them to Jaeger. The result is one of Elgar's most exquisite works (re-garding the two suites as one work) and is crucial to any real under-standing of the sort of person he was, as well as providing the strongest possible evidence of the early manifestation of his genius. The hand of a fifty-year-old master of his craft is upon the music as we know it now, of course, but the original thoughts, as the sketchbooks show, are not much altered.

The first suite begins with an Overture, bright and open-hearted and with a cantabile tune which suggests both the first subject of the Violin Concerto and its related theme in the finale of the same work:

Ex. 8

Ex. 9
Concerto (finale)

The Serenade has a clarinet melody over a lilting accompaniment for strings; the Minuet is an affectionate tribute to Handel in a manner that transcends pastiche: there is nothing of Haydn or Mozart in it, nor of Purcell; 'Sun Dance' has stylish and fluent woodwind writing not unlike the 'Dorabella' variation, sprightly until the central waltz and with virtuoso use of the harp near the end; with 'Fairy Pipers' we move into a darker world. It seems oddly titled, perhaps because we are conditioned to 'Pipes of Pan', and anyone who expects high woodwind tooting will be disappointed. Two clarinets in thirds play their evocative theme over a halting Bizet-like string accompaniment; this changes to a yearning of the strings which is not far away from the rarefied atmosphere of the introduction to Part II of *Gerontius*. This mood is continued into the 'Slumber Scene' (for strings), an exquisitely tender movement which ranks among quintessential Elgarian examples of his 'withdrawn' style. The last number, 'Fairies and Giants', is slightly Tchaikovskyan in its tarantella rhythm for the Fairies. The Giants – brass and bassoons, with unison strings playing detached crotchets – sound like a parody of the 'Dies irae' theme, which may well have been intended as a joke by the young Elgar.

The second suite has perhaps fewer deep moments, but the scoring is even more fluent and apposite to the nature of the themes. It begins with a March, not a fat fruity one but tense and hesitant with a faster trio. This has a rhythm which trips and skips along rather as children do, hands linked. 'The Little Bells' is a vivacious scherzino, again with a middle section in contrasted mood. It was this trio, a tender wistful strain, that Elgar put to effective use in the *Starlight Express* music, written for Algernon Blackwood's play in 1915. 'Moths and Butterflies' is Tchaikovskyan ballet music and 'Fountain Dance' elegant and picturesque. The suite ends with 'The Tame Bear' and 'Wild Bears', the former an elusive piece, its poignant mood engendered by plagal cadences, and the latter a romp which is also one of Elgar's most exotic pieces of orchestration.

Composition of *The Wand of Youth* was therapy for Elgar in 1907. He had just returned from a tour of the United States, an experience he never enjoyed, his eyes were troubling him, as they frequently did, and he was in one of his black moods. 'I see nothing ahead', he told one friend, and to Jaeger he wrote the recurrent refrain, 'I take no interest whatever in music now ... music is off'. He edited his 'old boyish MSS', and when he had finished, his wife heard him playing a 'great beautiful tune', the beginning of what was to become the First Symphony.

Of the smaller works in similar vein to *The Wand of Youth,* the best is *Dream Children,* Op. 43, two pieces for small orchestra generated by Lamb's essay – 'We are less than nothing, and dreams. We are only what might have been'. What might have been! How it sounds like a knell through so much of Elgar's music. These 1902 pieces exactly capture the sentiment; the first (again, prominent clarinet and oboe) has violins in octaves, over a tonic pedal, reaching out for new keys with an effect that recalls the 'Romanza' Variation, a *locus classicus* for Elgar's sense of the irrecoverable past. No. 2 begins more cheerfully – *allegro piacevole* is always a guarantee of Elgarian smiles – and ends wistfully.

Variations on an Original Theme (Enigma), Op. 36

The history of this famous work is well known and needs only brief recapitulation. In it Elgar drew musical sketches of thirteen of his friends (one of them his wife) and added a self-portrait as finale. Although the friends are disguised by initials or pseudonyms, their identities have long since been revealed. The Enigma is twofold: the theme itself, as heard at the outset, and 'through and over the whole set [of variations] another and larger theme "goes", but is not played'. It is the second enigma, the unplayed theme, that has attracted speculation and guesswork, from 'God Save the King' to 'Auld Lang Syne' and even 'Ta-ra-ra-boom-de-ay'. Or is the theme merely 'friendship' or a musical cryptogram? Probably no one will ever know. Elgar's strongest clue was that it was so well known he was surprised no one had guessed it. Might it not merely be a simple scale? He told 'Dorabella', whose real christian name was Dora, that she *'of all people'* ought to have guessed right. Why she? Doh-ray, perhaps. Or a secret reference to *Così fan tutte*, from which he took her pet name Dorabella? The first Enigma is less difficult. The theme surely represents Elgar himself, the constant factor in the whole work, viewing his friends through his, the theme's, eyes. For him, as he admitted later when he used it again in *The Music Makers* (1912), it represented the loneliness of the creative artist. He also referred to the Enigma as a 'dark saying', which again suggests Elgar's view of himself ('just like me and my influence on everybody – always evil'). I have suggested elsewhere* that the opening bars represent the name 'Edward Elgar' in natural speech-rhythm, for this is a procedure that might well have appealed to him. He signed letters with this phrase, and he used a similar device a few years later in *In the South* where this theme for violins

Ex. 10

was suggested by the name of the town Moglio, a name that amused him and his daughter Carice.

Elgar sent his manuscript score to Hans Richter in Vienna and the great Wagnerian conductor put the *Variations* into his next London concert on 19 June 1899. They were an immediate success and have become a classic. Here the Elgar of the salon music put his mastery of the short, highly polished, epigrammatic *moment musical* to its most perfect use in a skilfully designed structure and on a highly imaginative level. The contrast between individual variations and the grouping of the variations – dignified introduction followed by several short sketches leading to the

* *Portrait of Elgar* (O.U.P., 1968).

central slow movement (Nimrod) followed by a delicate intermezzo and an exuberant scherzo, with two extremely poetic
variations as an emotional climax before the assertive finale – are
on the same level of artistic and technical finesse as Brahms's
Variations on a theme by Haydn:

Theme (Enigma) *Andante*. Two contrasted strains, major and
minor. It leads without a break into

Variation 1 (C.A.E. – Elgar's wife) *Andante*. A simple expansion
of the theme, with the second phrase in E flat, radiant and serene.

Variation 2 (H.D.S.-P.) *Allegro*. In 3/8 time. Hew Stewart-
Powell played chamber music with Elgar and the variation
mocks his 'characteristic diatonic run over the keys' before he
began to play. The basses have the first strain of the theme.

Variation 3 (R.B.T.) *Allegretto*. A caricature of R. B. Townshend's
portrayal of an old man in amateur theatricals. The second part
of the theme is here in F sharp major.

Variation 4 (W.M.B.) *Allegro di molto*. In 3/4 time and the minor
key, this portrays a country squire, W. M. Baker, reading out
the day's plans to his guests and leaving the room, inadvertently
banging the door. Woodwind represent some of the guests'
humorous reception of this tirade.

Variation 5 (R.P.A.) *Moderato*. Richard Arnold, son of Matthew,
is portrayed here in C minor as a serious conversationalist
(first part of theme in bass, 12/8) who lightened what he was
saying with witticisms (flute has second part of theme in 4/4).

Variation 6 (Ysobel) *Andantino*. This is Isabel Fitton, an amateur
violist who had difficulty with crossing the strings. The solo
viola also depicts her romantic charm.

Variation 7 (Troyte) *Presto*. The drums are Arthur Troyte Griffith's
'maladroit essays to play the pianoforte'. The brass interjections
are Elgar's attempts to make order out of chaos – in vain, as
the final slam indicates.

Variation 8 (W.N.) *Allegretto*. In G major. The initials stand for
Winifred Norbury but this tranquil variation is really a picture
of her eighteenth-century ouse, 'Sherridge'.

Variation 9 (Nimrod) *Adagio*. This is the noble portrait, in E flat,
which Elgar drew of his friend and encourager A. J. Jaeger
and records a talk about Beethoven's slow movements, hence
the suggestion of the *Pathétique* sonata in the opening bars.

Variation 10 (Dorabella) Intermezzo, *Allegretto*. There is no reference to the theme here. It comes as the perfect contrast to Nimrod, lowering the tension without lowering the quality of inventiveness. Dorabella was Elgar's nickname for Dora Penny, later Mrs Richard Powell.

Variation 11 (G.R.S.) *Allegro di molto*. In G minor after the Intermezzo's G major. It depicts the Hereford organist George Sinclair's bulldog Dan swimming in the Wye and scrambling on to the bank with a rejoicing bark.

Variation 12 (B.G.N.) *Andante*. A moving tribute to the devoted friendship of Basil Nevinson, an amateur cellist.

Variation 13 (* * *) Romanza, *Moderato*. This marvellous variation is a seascape, with the drums representing the throb of a liner's engines and the clarinet quoting from Mendelssohn's overture *Calm Sea and Prosperous Voyage*. Elgar said it referred to Lady Mary Lygon's departure for Australia.

Variation 14 (E.D.U.) *Allegro*. This is Elgar himself (his wife's pet name for him was 'Edoo') and is his assertive retort to friends who were 'dubious and generally discouraging' about his future as a composer. C.A.E. is recalled, the theme is blared forth and there is a reference to Nimrod before the final exultant and emphatic bars.

A remarkable quality, built into the work as it were, is its perennial freshness – it always sounds new, as if the ink were hardly dry on the manuscript paper. The theme itself, so apt for variation yet so noble in itself, has two phrases: the first six bars for strings alone in G minor, with falling thirds and sevenths, and then a G major section, based on descending fourths and fifths. In the bass a counter-theme rises, and the effect of the entry of the wood-wind is but the first of many poetical moments.

Ex. 11

One aspect of the work that illuminates Elgar's craftsmanship is the smooth and inevitable way in which some of the Variations are linked. The glide into C.A.E. from the Introduction, for example, the elision between R.P.A., with its foreshadowing of both B.G.N. and Dorabella, and the civilised courtesies of Ysobel and her viola, the subtle change from W.N's grace and elegance to the solemn tribute to loyal friendship and mutual love of Beethoven that is Nimrod, the gentle merging of B.G.N's cello elegy into the mysterious Romanza, are accomplished with the simplest but most admirable means.

As for felicities of scoring, they are too numerous to survey in detail, but some of the finest are the bassoon solos in R.B.T., the colloquy of viola, horn and bassoon in Ysobel, the flashing strings, bright trumpets and eloquent timpani in Troyte, the muted violins, lisping clarinet and oboe, and solo viola in Dorabella (a flattering portrait from all accounts but rightly described by Thomas Dunhill* as 'unsurpassed in fragile daintiness by any piece of orchestral music one is able to recall'), and the woodwind counterpoint to the strings' gravities in B.G.N. Perhaps the gem of the set is the Romanza, in G major, switching to A flat and E flat, and incorporating the already mentioned quotation from Mendelssohn. The emotional state of the whole work has, up to this thirteenth variation, been if not detached at least balanced and poised, even the fervour of Nimrod being strongly controlled. Elgar's wistful vein does not appear until the closing bars of B.G.N. as they introduce the Romanza. Ostensibly this variation commemorates the departure of Lady Mary Lygon for Australia, but the clarinet quotation, played *molto espressivo* over throbbing timpani and strings and swelling brass, suggests the dark memory of some similar parting which tore Elgar to pieces. It is the most

* *Sir Edward Elgar* (Blackie, 1938).

intimate and impressive episode of the work, all the more power-ful for coming soon after the caperings of G.R.S.*

In their interplay of light and shade, sentiment and humour, and their startling clarity, the *Variations* are Elgar's orchestral masterpiece, almost flawless. The key scheme, with Nimrod resplendent in E flat major, is masterly. Only in the final self-portrait is the balance tipped slightly. Written, as Elgar said, when his friends were (as he usually complained they were) discouraging about his future, the opening of E.D.U. plainly tells them in musical terms to go to the devil, except for Nimrod (Jaeger, of Novello's) and Alice Elgar (C.A.E.), both of whose themes are recapitulated. Nimrod, an expressive *adagio* as Variation 9, now becomes grandioso, inflated, in the sometimes insensitive fashion in which Elgar treated some of his tenderest themes, in the revised ending extended at Richter's suggestion. The original ending is shown opposite.

The harmony of the *Enigma Variations* is principally diatonic, in marked contrast to the choral masterpiece *The Dream of Gerontius* which followed a year later. Although the Birmingham Festival chorus professed to find Elgar's music 'new' and difficult and Richard Strauss hailed him as 'progressive', it is unlikely that if Schumann and Mendelssohn had returned to earth they would have found much difficulty in coming to terms with Elgar's harmonic writing. The self-taught composer was content all his life with the models of his adolescence: Dvořák, Brahms, Wagner, Schumann.

There are few more convincing demonstrations in music of the assertion that if a composer has 'something to say' he can say it in the conventional language of his time and need not invent new harmonies and methods. Elgar's melodic gift was highly developed and remained fertile. His self-confidence and self-sufficiency were such that he seems to have taken only a passing

* Mr Leslie Sutton kindly told me of an amplified 'programme' for G.R.S. which he heard from Elgar's lips at Aberystwyth in the 1920s. In this version Dan saw a cat and chased it so vigorously that when it jumped on to the parapet of the Wye Bridge at Hereford he was unable to stop, cleared the parapet and splashed into the river. He then swam to the bank and gave one solitary bark of achievement or frustration. It fits the music.

The original ending of the Enigma Variations copied from the manuscript in the British Museum. (Reproduced by kind permission of Mrs. Elgar Blake and the Elgar Trustees.)

interest, if any at all, in the experiments of his near-contemporaries. Whatever he took from the air around him, it was not an echo of anything that Debussy, for instance, was writing, nor Ravel – he thought them both anaemic. The bitonality that interested Holst and Vaughan Williams passed him by. He was disappointed by Stravinsky's *Fire Bird* and *Petrushka*. If Schoenberg's atonal revolution impinged upon him at all, there is no record of his ever having commented upon it. On the whole he was uninterested by any of these developments, practically or theoretically. He did not need them. His own enthusiasms were for his elders; among his juniors Richard Strauss, Puccini and Delius held pride of place. Bach's Double Violin Concerto, Verdi's *Requiem*, Saint-Saëns's *Le Rouet d'Omphale*, Wagner's *Siegfried Idyll*, Liszt's *Les Préludes*, the music of Suppé and of Handel – these were among his varied favourites.

Four Tone-Poems

In an ill-considered and apparently unprepared digression during his Birmingham lecture on Brahms's Third Symphony, Elgar drew an unfortunate division between 'absolute' music and the programmatic, coming down heavily on the side of the absolute. People were quick to point out that much of Elgar's music was descriptive, and he in reply modestly declined to class himself with the Beethoven of the Fifth Symphony. It is a false kind of comparison, like saying that opera is a higher form of art than the symphony or vice versa. Most of Elgar's music has a descriptive basis, even in the 'absolute' forms of symphony and concerto. And between 1890 and 1913 he produced four works which are avowedly programmatic. Although three of them are classed as concert overtures they are in reality tone-poems.

OVERTURE, FROISSART, OP. 19

This was Elgar's first large-scale work for full orchestra, composed in 1890 at the request of the Worcester Festival committee, and its accomplishment is remarkable – 'shameless in its rude young health' was Elgar's description of it some years later, suggesting that he was by then well aware how far he had outgrown its gaucheries. But there was no other composer in England in 1890 who handled the orchestra with such assurance and ease. This is the best feature of *Froissart*. It is interesting today only as showing Elgar emerging from the chrysalis. So much is prophetic and characteristic, and yet it is for long stretches un-Elgarian.

The motto of the work – Keats's 'When Chivalry lifted up her lance on high' – and its literary origin in a conversation in Sir Walter Scott's *Old Mortality* about the historian Jean Froissart's chivalrous qualities are the first manifestations of this consciously 'noble' strain in Elgar. Typical of him are the profusion of themes – five in the introductory section – and the use of sequences, rising arpeggios, crotchet-quaver rhythms. The best of the themes bear the unmistakable signature of their composer, but the use to which they are put in the weak and too lengthy development section shows inexperience and the half-digested influences of Dvořák, Weber, Brahms and Schumann. The seed of the *Pomp and Circumstance* marches is in the exposition:

Ex. 12

The restraint with which the work is scored is notable. It is high spirited but never strident; and its vitality prevents its total eclipse by the much finer works that soon followed.

OVERTURE, COCKAIGNE (IN LONDON TOWN), OP. 40

Elgar's finest overture was written in 1900–1901 within the shadow of the depression caused by the failure of *Gerontius*, of which it betrays no sign. It is a tone-picture of turn-of-the-century London, picturesque, romantic, humorous, not a bar too long, scored with delicacy, panache and consummate ease. 'Honest, healthy, humorous, and strong but not vulgar', was how Elgar described his intentions in a letter to Richter, and he achieved them. There is no specific programme: various themes represent aspects of London and its inhabitants – the cheeky Cockneys, the dignified squares, the lovers in the parks, the City churches, a military procession and a less splendid band (perhaps the Salvation Army, it has been rather unfairly suggested).

Each vignette is dovetailed into the next – note, for instance, the hint on clarinets of the approach of the procession while the lovers' music is dying down. (The military-band episode might well be a memory of the Diamond Jubilee procession of 1897. There is the same sense of crowd excitement as is conveyed in the Coronation scene of *Falstaff*, and the chimes of bells – on the brass – would hardly be rung for any ordinary band.) The lyrical theme, nobilmente, representing the Londoner (Ex. 15), is among Elgar's best broad melodies; snatches of woodwind pointillisme abound delightfully; the bright sound of two cornets is reserved for the right brash moment (giving a hint to Vaughan Williams for his *London Symphony*); there is an episode of high romance as a solo horn, with accompanying strings, transcends the pictorial imagery and fixes the universal vision of a time that must fade. Like Brahms's *Academic Festival* overture, *Cockaigne* begins quietly, scherzando, and ends in a blaze of good fellowship.

OVERTURE, IN THE SOUTH (ALASSIO), OP. 50

The Elgars spent December 1903 and January 1904 in Italy, staying first at Bordighera and later at the Villa S. Giovanni, Alassio. It had been an open secret for some time that Elgar was at work on a symphony which he had promised to Richter after a Manchester performance of *Cockaigne* in 1901, but progress was slow and fitful: it was incubating, but no more. In March 1904 at Covent Garden an Elgar Festival of three concerts by Richter and the Hallé was arranged, a unique tribute to an English composer. Naturally the organisers hoped for the first performance of the symphony, and one newspaper even announced that this would take place. But in the January Elgar had told them that the symphony was 'impossible' and in its place he promised a concert overture, *In the South*, which he had written at Alassio as an attempt to recapture 'the thoughts and sensations of one beautiful afternoon in the Vale of Andora'. The music, therefore, is frankly descriptive and also has a literary basis in the quotations from Tennyson and Byron which Elgar wrote on the manuscript, of which the most significant is

> ... a land
> Which *was* the mightiest in its old command
> And *is* the loveliest ...
> Wherein were cast ...
> ... the men of Rome!
> Thou art the garden of the world.

History and landscape, in fact, are the programme of this rich and resonant tone-poem.

Some good judges, now that the work has taken a place in the repertoire after years of comparative neglect, consider that it is the finest of Elgar's shorter works. It certainly has superb passages – nothing in the whole of Elgar is more thrilling than the leaping opening (written five years earlier to illustrate the bulldog Dan of Variation 11 'triumphant after a fight'), divided strings and triumphant brass crowning all – but the development of the profusion of themes lacks the concision that gives *Cockaigne* its crisp authority. When this effervescent opening has run its course there is a calmer episode, pastoral and reflective, with the 'Moglio' theme (Ex. 10) as an answer to the shepherd's piping (clarinet). After the calm beauty of this section, evocative of the 'palm, orange blossom, olive, aloe, maize and vine' of Tennyson's lines, the music becomes agitated and lumbers into the Roman section, an impressive and astonishing grandioso section in A flat minor containing some of the boldest harmonies Elgar ever employed, as he recalls past grandeur, coupled with an awareness of its ugly aspect (slave-labour), and paints what he called 'the relentless and domineering onward force of the ancient day, and ... a sound-picture of the strife and wars, the "drums and tramplings" of a later time'. Strings and brass at their most sonorous convey the tramplings, the whole passage being inspired by the ruins of the viaduct at Turbia. Elgar builds a very brilliant passage on this striding theme and, as masterfully as in the *Variations,* merges it, via muted strings, into the second episode, the *canto popolare.* Perhaps intentionally saluting Berlioz, he gives this haunting tune

(original, but thoroughly Italian in spirit) to the solo viola –
'Edward in Italy':

Ex. 13

It sounds even more expressive as a horn solo, but when it has
returned, over a drum-roll, on the viola and has huskily reached
its end, there is a hiatus and Elgar goes back to the beginning of
the overture for a formal recapitulation. Thenceforward it may be
thought that Elgar's inspiration burns at less than its brightest and
one may think that his sense of obligation to the Covent Garden
Festival (and to its originator, his friend Frank Schuster, to whom
In the South is dedicated) led him to inflate the work beyond its
proper length.* It is all very decorative, but more than a whit contrived until the beautiful passage where a nobilmente theme from
the opening is transformed into a slow, gentle 6/4 melody before
being worked up to a final climax with strings, brass and glockenspiel in the ascendant. 'I *love* it: it's alive!' Elgar said, and no one
will contradict that.

FALSTAFF, SYMPHONIC STUDY IN C MINOR WITH TWO INTERLUDES IN A MINOR

The last of Elgar's tone-poems is one of his great masterpieces,
although it has weaknesses and perhaps does not wholly deserve
the unstinted praise bestowed on it by those who prefer its in-
tellectual literary subject-matter to the outpouring of the two
symphonies. It was completed in time for the Leeds Festival of
October 1913, where it had a cool reception, and was for many
years a rarity. Elgar recorded it in his last years, but it was so
infrequently performed in public that he once resorted to sending
a score to Beecham, asking him to consider conducting it. Sir
Thomas never bothered to reply.

The idea of a work about Falstaff had been in Elgar's mind since

*I have heard some performances that dispel these doubts.

1902. He was a lover of Shakespeare and extremely knowledge-able about him. The analytical note he wrote for the first per-formance displays his erudition and his close acquaintance with the commentators on Shakespeare's plays. (To digress: you have only to read Elgar's Birmingham lectures* to discover that his literary knowledge was deep and esoteric. And he was irritated by Harley Granville-Barker's *Winter's Tale* production when Autolycus was made to hide his face when he mentioned going about with troll-my-dames, 'suggesting', Elgar said, 'that he was thinking of improper women – it means a sort of gambling bagatelle board'.)

It was to be expected that Elgar would prefer the Falstaff of the historical plays to the 'caricature' in *The Merry Wives of Windsor*, and that he would particularly fix on Maurice Morgann's inter-pretation of Falstaff as a man of incongruities, 'a knight, a gentle-man and a soldier'. Typical, too, that the aspects of Falstaff which Elgar illustrates are those with which he felt a personal affinity, so that the work is yet another chapter of musical autobiography – these are his literary 'friends pictured within'. In the Gadshill escapade Elgar no doubt remembered the 'japes' of his youth with friends like Hubert Leicester (the time, for example, when he stood in for a curfew ringer at St Helen's Church, Worcester, and, being supposed to ring the day of the month, in his exuber-ance rang September 35): typical of Elgar that he should seize upon Falstaff's statement that he was page to the Duke of Norfolk not, as Verdi did, for a display of bubbling spirits, but as a means of recalling 'what might have been' in a violin solo that holds the freshness of boyhood in its wide intervals: Falstaff becomes one of the 'Dream Children'. Then, the march to the West Country and 'the fields and apple-trees' parallels Elgar's own delight in the countryside of his birth. There is subtlety, too, in the treatment of Prince Hal, whose theme is very nearly a parody of an Elgarian 'courtly' theme and from which Elgar withholds his accolade of nobilmente, perhaps, as a contemporary English composer has suggested to me, because he foreshadows all the way through the Hal music the man who will eventually disown the 'fool and jester'.

Falstaff is in one continuous movement but its title of 'sym

* See *A Future for English Music*.

phonic study' is abundantly justified by its design – exposition, development, recapitulation, with scherzo-like episodes and the equivalent of a slow movement, and, at the end, a symphonic epilogue of touching intensity when Falstaff on his deathbed recalls his past to music that is founded on the interlude in Shallow's orchard. 'He babbled of green fields.' And Elgar on his deathbed: 'I lie here hour after hour thinking of our beloved Teme – surely the most beautiful river that ever was.' There are four principal divisions: Falstaff and the Prince; the Boar's Head and the Gadshill robbery; Falstaff's march to Gloucestershire, the battle, and his return to London to greet Henry V; the King's progress to Westminster Abbey, his banishment of Falstaff, and Falstaff's death. The first section is mainly expository. The Falstaff theme, appropriately fat and luxuriant, is almost as fine an invention for characterisation by variation as the Enigma itself

Ex. 14

Allegro

and it and its variants are heard throughout the work, binding it into a unity: staccato for the Gadshill exploit, fugato at a moment of discomfiture, distorted for drunkenness, augmented for sleep and death. Counterpoint plays its usual apt role; also examples of theme transformation, notably the metamorphosis of the shambling march of Falstaff's bucolic recruits to the blithe song of greeting to the apple-orchards, to be followed by the interlude in Shallow's orchard where Elgar, scorning any resort to folk-song quotation, exactly captures the 'sadly-merry' mood of the countryside by alternating pipe and tabor with the passage for muted violas and cellos which eventually introduces the death of Falstaff.

The orchestration is probably Elgar's finest, since it is perhaps on a more ambitious scale than that of the *Enigma Variations*. It is the inevitability of Elgar's scoring that is so wondrous – the music, one feels, could never be scored in any other way; it grows from the instruments. 'I never have had to alter anything', he told Jaeger in 1898, and in his Birmingham lecture on orchestration he said: 'I find it impossible to imagine a composer creating a musical idea without defining inwardly and simultaneously the exact means of its presentation.' This is specially true in *Falstaff*, where the range of instrumental colour is extraordinary, achieved without the use of any out-of-the-way instruments and giving a moment of glory to every instrument from first violin to side-drum.

Where the work is open to criticism is in the too frequent reliance on sequences, which amounts to a mannerism in the Gads-hill episode, and in certain failures of characterisation. The women are idealised beyond anything that Falstaff or anyone else ever met in a London tavern, and the insistence on the noble side of Falstaff's character tips the scale towards the melancholy side of Elgar's. His theme representing his 'cheerful look and pleasing eye' is chromatic, dark-coloured by violas and cor anglais. Tovey thought it was meant to be Falstaff 'blown up like a bladder with sighing and grief', and one has every sympathy with him. Yet in the long view these are small blemishes on a broad and expansive canvas which can be claimed as one of the most vivid, subtle and convincing unifications of literature and music.

Pomp and Circumstance

Much has been misunderstood about Elgar, but nothing quite so much as his directive 'nobilmente'. This is usually loosely quoted as though it referred exclusively to Elgar's parade-ground manner or to passages where he wanted an element of pageantry or pompous rhetoric. But a study of his scores will show how carefully and often he reserved it for very particular melodies and phrases, nearly always those which express what he himself called his 'stately sorrow' and Yeats called his 'heroic melancholy'. Elgar was a precise user of words, and when he required an effect of blatancy, or assertive emphasis, he nearly always used grandioso, as in the finale of the *Enigma Variations* and the appearance of

King Henry V 'gorgeous as the sun at mid-summer' in *Falstaff,* and in the closing pages of *In the South* and the First Symphony, where the motto-theme which stood in Elgar's mind for high moral qualities and is marked nobilmente e semplice at its first appearance is now blared forth, despite the attempts by off-beat rhythms to undermine its triumphant progress. The first use of nobilmente, so far as I have been able to discover, was in the *Cockaigne* overture of 1901, where it lends a stately lyricism to the broad theme representing the Londoner:

Ex. 15

Thereafter it came more and more to be restricted to music which we know was rich in personal emotional significance for Elgar. For instance, he wrote no more intimate work than the Violin Concerto, that repository of his secret longings: the first entry of the violin, a moment of grave poetry, and its final regretful recall at the end of the cadenza, are marked nobilmente, and so is one of the most emotional themes of the second movement.

The slow movement of the Second Symphony was inspired by the death of a close friend, A. E. Rodewald, and the whole work, as will be seen, is full of associations with friends and places he loved. Much of it, and much elsewhere in the work, is marked nobilmente, not as has too often been wrongly deduced because the Symphony is dedicated to the memory of Edward VII, but because of its genesis as 'the passionate pilgrimage of a soul'. The second subject of the finale, for example, a nobilmente tune, began life with the inscription 'Hans [Richter] himself', to whom Elgar once wrote, 'You have from me all the love and reverence one man can feel for another'. A far cry from empty rhetoric.

The cello's introductions to the first and last movements of the Cello Concerto, another work in which the deepest feelings are engaged, are marked nobilmente; so is the solemn E flat tune at the climax of the exposition of *In the South,* dedicated to Frank Schuster – 'I have said in music', Elgar wrote after his beloved Frankie's death, 'what I felt, long ago – in F's own overture . . .

in the key he loved most I believe, warm and joyous, with a grave radiating serenity.' The end of the first movement of the String Quartet is nobilmente, so is the lyrical 'Welsh tune' of the *Introduction and Allegro* for strings (Ex. 3). One bar of the introduction to the Angel's 'Behold my servant whom I have chosen' in *The Apostles* is nobilmente, and it is used at four vital points in *The Kingdom*: at the climax of 'O ye priests' when the chorus sing of standing before the congregation to minister unto them, in Peter's great solo when he reminds the disciples that they were witnesses to Christ's Resurrection, the five last bars of Part III referring to Christ's glorification, and at the ecstatic climax of Mary's 'The sun goeth down'. *Gerontius*, like the *Enigma Variations*, came before Elgar had 'hit on' nobilmente and it is worth noting that for the music which he would surely have marked nobilmente a year later – the Priest's 'Proficiscere' – he had to be wordily precise: solenne e con elevazione.

All this is a necessary prelude to a discussion of the set of five *Pomp and Circumstance* marches, Op. 39, which Elgar published between 1901 and 1930. Those are the three words most associated with Elgar's name in the public's mind, and it has sometimes seemed that many superficial commentators on his music have equated nobilmente with pomp and circumstance.* In fact only two of the five contain this direction, No. 4 (the tune of the trio) and No. 5 (again, the trio). In the famous No. 1, the great melody which at Edward VII's prompting became 'Land of Hope and Glory', is marked legato e cantabile at its first appearance and molto maestoso at its repetition. It did not become nobilmente in the *Coronation Ode* (1902), the only use of the term in that work being at the pianissimo episode in the first movement when the chorus sing the words 'All that hearts can pray'.

Elgar felt no need to apologise for his popular marches, nor need his adherents today. What we owe him is the effort of stripping away from them the political accretions and listening to them simply as music. I will not propound that we will find as much of the secret Elgar as in *The Wand of Youth*, but their relevance to his larger works is nonetheless considerable. He made no distinctions in his own mind between parts of his output, and

* The basses' 'The march triumphal thunders' in the notorious Triumph Scene in Rome from *Caractacus* (1898) is marked pomposamente.

it is self-evident that the trio of March No. 1 is the cousin of the opening of the First Symphony: it is even rather a melancholy tune, scored on its first appearance in sombre colours. The march rhythm haunts the symphonies in a distraught, sometimes ghostly or fantastic, fashion, very much as it does the symphonies of Mahler – notably, for example, in the second movement of the First Symphony. The opening section of March No. 1 is a fine example of Elgar's taut-reined restlessness, a splendid contrast to the spaciousness of the central melody. A similar contrast is to be found in No. 4, perhaps the most 'ceremonial' of the set. The best of the five is probably No. 2, which resembles a Schubert *marche militaire* in spirit. Its key is A minor and that of No. 3 is C minor. The latter has a slightly sinister opening, with Elgar's characteristic 'thumps' off the beat, and becomes jovial. The trio, over a marching bass, is lyrical and light and merges deliciously into the repetition of the opening music. The ending is too wholesome to be described as nightmarish but there is a detectable sense of frenzy in the coda. March No. 5, not published until 1930, is in his Massenet-ballet manner, theatrical and gay, its trio sounding a deeper note, and the piece ending with a superb coda in which the brilliance of the orchestration is paramount. These are the greatest concert marches ever written or likely to be.

Elgar first won popular national acclaim in 1897 with the *Imperial March*, Op. 32, written for Queen Victoria's diamond jubilee. This is a strangely muted piece, despite its pomposo opening, glowing rather than glittering. The *Coronation March,* Op. 65, of 1911 includes material discarded from a proposed *Rabelais* ballet and, like the *Empire March* of 1924, is rhetoric, not oratory. The most poetic and haunting of all Elgar's marches is the Funeral March, Op. 42, which he wrote in 1901 for the play *Grania and Diarmid* by W. B. Yeats and George Moore. Its extraordinary atmosphere is attributable to modality (Aeolian) and its trio, marked nobilmente, is of all its kind most nearly related to the symphonic Elgar, both in breadth and beauty. It was this music that Yeats described as 'wonderful in its heroic melancholy'.

Elgar's penchant for the march, first traceable in the *Pas redoublé* of 1882, carried over into his larger works. He himself regarded his music as all of a piece and was understandably irritated by the squeamish critics who divided him into two Elgars, serious and salon. Tunes like *Chanson de nuit* show how close is the melodic outline of Elgar's small pieces to some of the great melodies of his major works. Similarly, features of march rhythm and his ceremonial style occur in the big works. Chromatic scales for the brass occur in the First Symphony and the Cello Concerto as well as in the *Coronation March*. Marching crotchets in the bass begin the First Symphony as well as the trios of several marches. The main theme of the finale of the Violin Concerto is a march tune

Ex. 16

and so, after all, is the processional 'Go forth' in *The Dream of Gerontius*. As for the highly characteristic thump on the off-beats, to be found in some of the Powick quadrilles, this can be heard not only in *Pomp and Circumstance*, No. 3, but in the two symphonies, in *Falstaff* and in the Cello Concerto. The beginning of the finale of the Cello Concerto is in fact a textbook passage for the study of all the main features of Elgar's march style within the context of a generally restrained concerto movement.

As Elgar pointed out in his 1905 lectures, 'vulgarity in the course of time may be refined. Vulgarity often goes with inventiveness . . . but the commonplace mind can never be anything but commonplace. . . . An Englishman will take you into a large room, beautifully proportioned, and will point out to you that it is white – all over white – and somebody will say "What exquisite taste". You know in your own mind, in your own soul, that it is not taste at all, that it is the want of taste, that is mere evasion. English music is white, and evades everything.'

There are no white rooms in Elgar's music.

Music for Strings

Of all Elgar's earlier works the finest, and the most eloquent of his ultimate capability, is the *Serenade* for strings, in E minor, Op. 20, written in 1892, or perhaps rewritten then, because it seems extremely likely that his *Three Pieces for String Orchestra* (Spring Song, Elegy and Finale), performed at Worcester in May 1888, are the *Serenade* in another form. 'I like 'em, the first thing I ever did', Elgar said of the *Three Pieces,* and he expressed a similar affection for the *Serenade*. Already there is complete mastery of the medium, and the Elgarian hallmarks are more firmly stamped on the music than on any passage in *Froissart*. 'Really stringy in effect', Elgar himself told Jaeger with complete accuracy; this is at once evident from the opening pages, with the dotted figure in the violas and the highly characteristic main theme:

Ex. 17

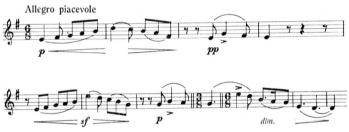

To call this carefully wrought and emotionally delicately-poised movement salon music, as has been done, is grossly to underestimate its quality. But perhaps the central *larghetto* in C major is so powerful and profound an apparition in a lightweight early work that it too easily overshadows its surroundings. Its sustained mood of elegiac nobility is the strongest pointer in early Elgar to the writer of the slow movements of the symphonies. It takes a great composer to know how to round off a short work containing so eloquent a centrepiece, and the brief finale, hesitant to break the spell at first and then recalling the opening movement and the dotted viola theme, is both delicate and to the point.

His next work for strings was the masterly *Introduction and Allegro*, Op. 47, first performed in March 1905. Its origin is interesting and, as so often with Elgar's music, topographical. In August 1901 he spent a holiday in Cardiganshire where he heard a choir singing on the other side of a bay and made sketches for a 'Welsh overture'. Three years later he heard a similar song 'far down our own Valley of the Wye'. This reminded him of his 'Welsh tune' and he incorporated it in the work for strings which he was writing at the behest of Jaeger, who had suggested 'a real bring-down-the-house torrent of a thing such as Bach could write' as an offering for the recently-formed London Symphony Orchestra. Elgar suggests the eighteenth-century concerto grosso by employing a string quartet whose role, however, is not to act primarily as soloists, but to provide moments of contrast or to blend with the full strings. 'No working-out part,' he wrote to Jaeger in January 1905, 'but a devil of a fugue instead. G major & the said divvel in G minor with all sorts of japes and counterpoint.' In his programme-note he wrote: 'The work is really a tribute to that sweet borderland where I have made my home,' i.e. Herefordshire.

Every means of exploiting the power and variety of stringed instruments is used in this concise, free-ranging yet almost classically designed work. Open strings, triple stopping, grace notes, pizzicato, ponticello tremolo, use of mutes – all these devices are called into play. But it is the material on which they are used that is so striking: instead of the usual profusion of themes Elgar based the whole work on three short statements; and it is paradoxical that whereas the music never sounds formally organised – 'free fantasia' would be an apt description – it is, despite the absence of a development section, as closely argued a work as Elgar ever invented. The three themes are:

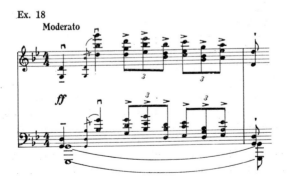

Ex. 18

Moderato

followed by this typical soaring *allegretto* theme (played by the quartet) over which in the manuscript Elgar wrote a quotation from *Cymbeline*, 'Smiling with a sigh':

Ex. 19

followed by this in the bass:

Ex. 20

Then the solo viola introduces the 'Welsh' theme already quoted as Ex. 3. Having propounded these ideas, Elgar begins the *allegro* section with Ex. 19, now in G major and sounding much less wistful. This is followed by a conversational interchange of repeated staccato semiquavers between quartet and main body of strings, culminating in an elaborate restatement of Ex. 18, after which the cut and thrust of the music is at its most exciting. This dramatic passage ends diminuendo with a poetical version of the Welsh tune, played in unison by the quartet, to a shimmering accompaniment and with a marvellously effective use of pizzicato. A pause, and the fugue begins, playful and prancing, with a pendant theme which is Ex. 20 from the Introduction. The fugue is, in effect, a kind of scherzo and when it has run its course, the *allegro* is recapitulated and the Welsh tune returns, nobilmente, richly harmonised and with all the sonority of which strings are capable. A final reference to Ex. 19 and this masterly composition, equalled among English works for strings only by Vaughan Williams's *Tallis Fantasia,* ends with one very final pizzicato chord.

Elgar wrote two other short works for strings. The *Elegy,* Op. 58, was written in 1909 in memory of a Junior Warden of the Worshipful Company of Musicians and is a short, solemn piece in the mood of 'Nimrod' and the *larghetto* of the *Serenade*. In 1914, a few days after war was declared, Sir Henry Wood conducted the first performance of *Sospiri*, Op. 70, for strings, harp and organ, dedicated to Elgar's close friend, the orchestral violinist W. H. Reed. Though short, this is one of his most affecting and deeply-felt utterances, expressive (via the interval of a seventh, yet again) of a mood of anguished desolation not far removed from the Mahlerian world. There is a heart-cry here which must have sounded strangely out of key with the mood of August 1914 but four years later was to find fuller, though less concentrated, expression in the finale of the Cello Concerto.

The Concertos

Elgar wrote two concertos, plus a small *Romance* for bassoon and orchestra, Op. 62, and left one, for pianoforte, unfinished. Those for violin, Op. 61, and for cello, Op. 85, rank not only among his greatest works but among the greatest of their kind. In style they provide a remarkable contrast, the former being expansive and magniloquent (although it is intimate in expression) and the latter compact, epigrammatic and disillusioned.

The Violin Concerto was tentatively begun in the summer of 1907, taken up again in 1909 and completed a year later. 'It's *good!* awfully emotional! too emotional but I love it,' Elgar wrote to his friend Frank Schuster during its composition. 'This concerto is *full* of romantic feeling – I should have been a philanthropist if I had been a rich man.' It was a work of intense personal significance for Elgar. It is dedicated to Fritz Kreisler, who gave the first performance on 10 November 1910, but on the score is a quotation in Spanish: 'Aquí está encerrada el alma de . . . . .' ('Herein is enshrined the soul of . . . . .').

Those five dots represent another Elgarian enigma. Whose soul is enshrined in this impassioned music, wild with all regret for what might have been, an idyllic idealisation? Elgar admitted that the 'soul' was feminine. Does it refer, like the Romanza variation, to some relationship, buried and irrecoverable, in Elgar's youth? He gave no clue. Lady Elgar is said by 'Dorabella' to have told her that the five dots stood for 'Pippa', the pet name by which the American Mrs Julia Worthington was known to the

Elgars; Elgar is said to have been in love with her. There is no documentary evidence to support Dorabella's contention, whereas there is plenty that the Concerto was specially associated with another of Elgar's women friends, Alice Stuart-Wortley, wife of an M.P. and daughter of the painter Millais. Elgar's name for her was 'Windflower', and he called some of the themes in the Concerto 'Windflower themes' and all his life referred to the work in his letters to her as 'our own concerto', sometimes beginning letters with a quotation from it. Whether Mrs Stuart-Wortley was a substitute relationship for the real 'Soul' or the Soul herself, she was certainly left in no doubt by Elgar that the music of this Concerto was intended for her.

And what music! It embodies all of Elgar's intimate understanding of the nature of the violin and thereby places a huge strain on the soloist, who must not only be a virtuoso with stamina but also an exceptionally sensitive and intelligent interpreter, alert to every Elgarian nuance of rubato. He must have a big tone capable of dominating the orchestra at full blast, and must also be able to convey to the listener that he is lost in a private self-communing of peculiar intimacy. For this is wayward music, extrovert one minute, inward the next, constantly changing mood by the subtlest inflexions. It begins with a long classical orchestral tutti in which five principal themes are quickly stated before the first of them is repeated, first by the orchestra and then completed by the soloist – one of the most effective and haunting entries by the solo instrument to be found in any concerto. The soloist elaborates the five themes, shedding new light on them and transforming the second subject, which is almost 'thrown away' on its first entry, into one of Elgar's most moving themes (a real 'Windflower' theme, this one):

Ex. 21

Development and recapitulation follow a fairly conventional course, the music continually ranging through a wide variety of keys. The interplay between violinist and orchestra is on an heroic scale – none but the brave deserves the fair in this Concerto. The slow movement, *andante*, is in the remote key of B flat. It begins almost coolly, remote and under control, its song-like character having a quasi-ecclesiastical flavour. But this soon changes and the movement grows more and more passionate, in much the same way as Mary's 'The sun goeth down' in *The Kingdom* rises from controlled peace to a stormy affirmation of faith.

Some of the themes are nobilmente and dolce, the violin determining their character with a display of sustained and noble eloquence that lifts the music on to a plane which even Elgar rarely attained. He pits his soloist against the deep sonority of trombones and horns, but the effect is perfectly calculated to allow the violin's tone to remain dominant throughout.

The finale (*allegro molto*) is the most rhapsodical and elaborate movement, opening with the soloist's rapid ascending passages as a prelude to the strong *vivace* main theme, Ex. 16, one of Elgar's striding, martial tunes, and a further profusion of sub-sidiary themes, notably Ex. 9, all of which are vigorously de-veloped at some length and yet seem always to be merely the prelude to bigger things, as indeed they are. The soloist is called upon for pyrotechnics here as well as for commanding lyricism. One of the Concerto's finest interpreters, Yehudi Menuhin, has said that it 'should be sung' and even in the dazzling brilliance of the first section of the finale the need for a full singing tone from the soloist is essential. When the key of B major is reached, Elgar reintroduces one of the principal themes of the slow movement, its tempo adapted to that of the finale, and soloist and orchestra expound upon it until the finale's chief subjects return.

Then a change comes over the music. It goes into the tonic minor once more, and the instruments are thinned away until nothing is left except a muted horn. The strings begin a magical shimmering by means of Elgar's invention of pizzicato tremolando (obtained, he instructed, by 'thrumming' with the soft parts of three or four fingers across the strings) and we are launched on the long accompanied cadenza which is the heart and soul of the work and one of the most memorable episodes in violin literature. Here is enshrined the soul of the violin, as it recalls themes from

45

the first and second movements, musing on them, rhapsodising about them, caressing them, elaborating them, all the time accompanied by the orchestra, or just the thrumming strings, in a background of misty and mysterious harmony. The exquisite 'Windflower' theme (Ex. 21) returns. To quote Samuel Langford's superb description: 'Each time the opening phrase of melody is repeated it vanishes in a mysterious coruscation of ascending notes which suggest the swift passing of a beauty once cherished as the hope and sum of life.'

In the passage preceding the cadenza and in the cadenza itself Elgar demonstrates the close relationship of all the themes in the Concerto. The cadenza ends with the soloist playing once again the phrase with which he entered in the first movement, as though bidding it farewell. But there is no lingering. The brilliant music of the introduction to the finale returns and the work ends in triumph.

It could be that the model for both Elgar's concertos was the Cello Concerto of Dvořák. Apart from sharing the same key as the Violin Concerto, the Dvořák Concerto is on an almost equally grand and elaborate scale. In design the first movements of both works are remarkably similar, the slow movements are intimate, song-like meditations and the recollection of earlier themes in a passionate final cadenza is carried to even greater lengths in Elgar than in Dvořák and is further employed in the Elgar Cello Concerto. Elgar expressed his youthful admiration for Dvořák's orchestration in these words: 'No matter how few instruments he uses it never sounds thin.' But the converse is also true, and both Elgar and Dvořák in their B minor concertos use a symphonic orchestra with a richness and colour that never obscure the soloist.

Elgar's Cello Concerto, Op. 85, was composed ten years after the Violin Concerto but seems to belong to another age, another world. As indeed it does, for between these two works lies the cataclysm of the First World War, which swept away Europe's, England's and Elgar's high noon. 'Never glad confident morning again.' The war aged and anguished Elgar. Many of his friends and champions were Germans and he saw them become enemies or enemy aliens. He shared the exultant mood of 1914 enough to join the Special Constabulary in Hampstead and to compose *Carillon,* an orchestral background to the recitation of a patriotic

46

poem by the Belgian poet Cammaerts. He conducted a good deal.
He set three of Binyon's poems including 'For the Fallen' in a
choral work of grave beauty called *The Spirit of England*, and he
set four Kipling poems, *The Fringes of the Fleet,* and toured the
music-halls in 1917 conducting them.

Privately, though, he was ill and unhappy, homesick for Worcestershire. The deaths of old friends depressed him. He had
Ménière's disease of the ear which caused dizziness and headaches.
His financial anxieties were as acute as ever: 'I am more alone and
the prey of circumstances than ever before. . . . Everything good
and nice and clean and fresh and sweet is far away – never to
return.' In this mood one could do nothing with him, and his
wife realised that the only chance for him was to find some
country retreat where he could be quiet and alone just as he had
been at 'Birchwood', the cottage they had rented near Malvern
at the turn of the century and where Elgar had been happier than
at any other time in his life. She found 'Brinkwells', an oak-
beamed cottage near Fittleworth, Sussex, in 1917 and there Elgar
regained his strength and his appetite for composition.

He was an autumnal figure now, and his surroundings suited
his frame of mind. He occupied himself chopping wood and making
hoops for barrels and building bonfires. During 1918 he wrote
three chamber works – a violin sonata, string quartet and pianoforte quintet – in which a different, more restrained Elgar emerged.
He refused to set Binyon's *Peace Ode* – 'the whole atmosphere [of
the time] is too full of complexities for me to feel music to it', he
explained. 'I regret the appeal [in the poem] to the Heavenly
Spirit which is cruelly obtuse to the individual sorrow and sacrifice
– a cruelty I resent bitterly & disappointedly.' In this mood he
began work on the Cello Concerto, which was completed in the
summer of 1919 – 'a real large work and I think *good* & alive,'
he wrote to its dedicatees, Sir Sidney and Lady Colvin. It was
played for the first time by Felix Salmond and the London
Symphony Orchestra on 26 October 1919, a performance almost
as disastrous as the first *Dream of Gerontius* had been nineteen
years earlier. Elgar's rehearsal time was reduced by an hour
because of the selfishness of Albert Coates who was conducting
the rest of the concert and was anxious to secure a good performance of Skryabin's *Poem of Ecstasy*.

The Concerto begins with a nobilmente flourish for the soloist:

Ex. 22

a splendid, virile gesture which emphasises the contrast of the movement's main theme, a long, lulling tune, something like a slimmed-down version of Falstaff's theme. In its world-weary way it is the music of autumn smoke and falling leaves and it winds its way through the keys, interrupted only by a brief, slightly more energetic episode in 12/8 time which begins with a woodwind-cello dialogue. As the movement quietly ends there is a pizzicato reference to the introduction and after a pensive, hesitant trying-over of the main theme by the cellist, the quicksilver scherzo begins, although the movement is not called a scherzo by Elgar, simply *allegro molto*. Tovey called the movement 'impish' but there is a sinister, restless air hovering round the playfulness and more than a touch of sadness in the hesitant subsidiary theme:

Ex. 23

The movement requires the utmost precision from the soloist, particularly in the closing bars. The *adagio* that follows is very short (60 bars) and is based on a long melody divided into two phrases. The key is B flat, as in the *andante* of the Violin Concerto, but whereas that movement was rapturous, this is near to tragedy, a lament for thoughts that lie too deep for tears, perfectly suited to the cello at its most songfully sustained, and ending with a dominant cadence, as if the tonic key was too positive.

The finale begins with a cello recitative that links the intro-duction to the first movement with hints at the main subject of this quasi-rondo. When the movement gets under way the pre-war

Elgar returns – for the last time – with swaggering rumbustious themes, volleys of brass tone, bright colours, off-the-beat crashes. At one point (cues 59–61) Falstaff's bulk seems to loom up in the orchestra. But all is short-lived. Chromatic harmonies on the strings change the mood back to one of tragic portentousness, and an accompanied cadenza is based on a new theme which is a more desolate heart-cry even than *Sospiri*. At this point we are not far away from the 'sense of ruin' which pervades the first part of *The Dream of Gerontius*. The second phrase of the *adagio* theme is recalled, perhaps as consolation in despair, the introduction returns, and as the cello plunges to the depths a version of the main theme of the finale rushes the work to a hasty, unconvincingly high-spirited ending.

The Concerto is scored for double woodwind with optional piccolo, four horns, two trumpets, three trombones, optional tuba, timpani and strings. Elgar's use of this orchestra as background for so sonorous an instrument as the violoncello is continuously fascinating and is as memorable an example as any in his whole output of his superb and unfailing craftsmanship as an orchestrator. The dexterity and lightness of touch throughout the work are astonishing, yet there is never any suggestion that the music is lightweight. Take the opening of the Concerto: the cello nobilmente and fortissimo – supported by lower strings, clarinets and bassoons as contrast, and then the violas' meandering tune gradually reinforced by orchestral cellos, the soloist, clarinets and horns. Not until cue 5 is the full orchestra employed at a climax (without the soloist) and then only for six bars. The soloist is heard usually with strings as accompaniment or woodwind, rarely with the brass except for a bar or two from the horns.

In the scherzo Elgar is at his best and adopts almost a pointilliste technique to achieve an impression of fantasy and to highlight the solo instrument. While the cello, leggierissimo and brillante, scurries along or indulges in high tessitura, there are flecks of colour from woodwind, a chord from horns and trumpets, the barest of sustenance from the strings which are often divided and often pizzicato. Twice, when the tempo slackens and broadens, the orchestration thickens too, but by the end it is thinned down to a skeletal framework. For the *adagio,* the orchestra is reduced to strings, clarinets, bassoons and horns, with the strings having

D

the main burden of supporting the cello's lament. Elgar throws his main compositional weight behind the finale, which occupies as many pages of score as the other three movements together. He is careful in the dramatic opening to ensure that the cello takes the centre of the stage untrammelled by hangers-on. When the robust main theme gets under way, the brass are again silent altogether when the soloist is playing, or only a horn solo is allowed. One can observe from the look of the printed page how spare some of the writing is, yet the effect is of fullness. The central orchestral section of the movement at cue 61, with cello silent, is the only time after the opening that full forces are employed, and as the end is neared and the sense of tragedy increases, it is Elgar's wonderful writing for the orchestral strings that unerringly colours the mood of the music. For the last eight or nine bars soloist and full orchestra are combined for the first and only time in the Concerto.

In form this is the simplest of all Elgar's major works. It is also the least grandiloquent, for it cannot even muster as much rhetoric as the *Introduction and Allegro*. Although the actual quality of the melodic invention is less striking – or so it seems to me – than in the Violin Concerto and the Symphonies, its selectivity, its compactness and its unusual design, together with the immensely attractive appeal it holds out to an expressive soloist (but, essentially, a disciplined one, not prone to self-indulgence), give this Cello Concerto a nearly supreme place among examples of the genre and have won it admirers among those who find Elgar's robuster style a little overwhelming.

The *Romance* for bassoon, an instrument which Elgar could play, hardly deserves its neglect. Elgar explores the poetry of the instrument rather than its overworked capacity for broad humour, although wit is not lacking.

The Symphonies

In the *Musical Times* of March 1899 a paragraph appeared to the effect that among compositions by Elgar 'on the stocks' was a symphony for the Worcester Festival to be called the *Gordon*

Symphony because it would reflect the extraordinary career and character of General Gordon, 'his military achievements, his unbounded energy, his self-sacrifice, his resolution, his deep religious fervour'. This subject, the writer (Jaeger) suggested, afforded 'full scope for the exercise of Mr Elgar's genius'. Elgar and Jaeger had discussed the idea during 1898, Elgar first saying that he could not afford to write a symphony and in any case, if it was to be a Three Choirs commission, he would have to discover whether the Dean and Chapter would accept the subject for a Cathedral performance. But he admitted that 'the thing possesses me, but I can't write it down yet'. In February 1899 he wrote of 'making a shot at it', and evidently some of the work was sketched, because in October 1901, in a letter to the conductor Hans Richter, he spoke of 'the Symphony I am trying to write' and promised that it would be dedicated to Richter, adding 'but I have much to do yet'.

The Leeds Festival were anxious for the first performance of the work and, as has already been mentioned, the organisers of the Elgar Festival in 1904 hoped for a symphony as the climax of the three days. But nothing materialised. Elgar would not be hurried. It has been seen how he would 'brood' over material for years until the moment came when he was able to fit all the jigsaw pieces together and make a complete picture. He believed in inspiration as well as in hard work. In one of his Birmingham lectures he quoted with approval these lines by Alfred Hayes:

> He hears the music of his heart
> But knows not whence the breath is blown;
> It comes from regions far apart,
> With power beyond his own.
> A presence at his side alights,
> A whisper at his ear is heard;
> Amazed he takes the pen, and writes
> The inevitable word.

In the same lecture he gave perhaps another clue to his hesitancy about producing a symphony. Then, as now, there was much talk about the future of the symphony as an art-form. It was outdated, dead, some pundits declared: Brahms had finished it off. Tchaikovsky's and Sibelius's symphonies were considered unsymphonic, avant-garde composers like Debussy were showing no interest in the form; Mahler's works were unknown outside Germany and Austria and were in any case regarded as mammoth eccentricities; Richard Strauss had used the symphonic poem as his chief outlet. Elgar said (on 13 December 1905): 'I hold that the symphony without a programme is the highest development of art . . . . Because the greatest genius of our days, Richard Strauss, recognises the symphonic poem as a fit vehicle for his splendid achievements, some writers are inclined to be positive that the symphony is dead. Perhaps the form *is* somewhat battered by the ill-usage of some of its admirers, although some modern symphonies still testify to its vitality; but when the looked-for genius comes, it may be absolutely revived. . . . Just as in our day what has been called "Suburban Gothic" from its mere imitation and boldness gives us only a dismal amusement, so the symphony became the prey of the would-be sayer of wise things and fell into the same sort of suspicion.'

From this it is clear how much importance Elgar attached to the symphony. He knew how eagerly awaited was his first essay in the form and, sensitive to criticism as he was, he knew that his reputation would be severely mauled by a failure in this respect. By attempting a symphony in the traditional form in this climate of opinion, Elgar was declaring his faith not only in symphonic design but in himself. How much of the Gordon idea is present in the symphonies as we know them it is impossible to say. The long march-theme which opens and dominates the First Symphony has an heroic quality but there is evidence that it was composed in June 1907, when Elgar had presumably abandoned the idea of an overtly programmatic symphony. But, as will be elaborated later, both symphonies are 'about' something; however professorial Elgar's statements about 'absolute' music may have sounded, he remained a man and artist who was inspired by people and places, and his two symphonies are personal memorials of both. That they are also self-sufficient musical structures is the measure of his achievement. They belong in spirit with the symphonies of Mahler, another late-romantic who used music as an outlet for autobiography. Mahler's music sometimes seems to belong to the psychiatrist's couch; Elgar's sometimes belongs to the confessional. I emphasise the words 'in spirit' because technically and structurally there is little resemblance between Elgar and Mahler. Elgar's scoring is richer, his harmonies less prophetic of the next generation. But both tell us, in their different ways, of the transience of human life, the frailty of human emotions, the sadness of time passing. With Mahler the expression sometimes borders on neurosis. In Elgar there is a sturdier streak; his music is nervy but not neurotic.

SYMPHONY NO. I IN A FLAT, OP. 55

After the first performance of *The Kingdom* in 1906 Elgar wrote very little for a few months. He was ill and depressed, and it was only work on the boyhood music of *The Wand of Youth* during the summer of 1907, when he passed his fiftieth birthday, that seemed to revive his creative spirits. He wrote the start of a symphony, laid it aside, and went to Italy for the winter. There he completed the first movement, and on his return home worked almost uninterruptedly on the other three movements between June and September of 1908. He dedicated the symphony to Hans Richter, 'true artist and true friend', who conducted the first performance in Manchester on 3 December 1908. This and the London performance four days later were triumphs, the finest Elgar ever had. 'The greatest symphony of modern times', Richter called it, adding that the *adagio* was such as Beethoven might have written. The public clamoured to hear the work again, and in just over a year it received a hundred performances all over the world. Once again the Symphony had been revived by a master-composer.

Elgar told Ernest Newman that this was *not* the Gordon Symphony and to Walford Davies he was even more explicit: 'There is no programme beyond a wide experience of human life with a great charity (love) and a *massive* hope in the future.' This 'great charity' is perhaps what is conveyed by the opening of the Symphony, one of the most unusual and striking in the whole of music: over a quiet drum-roll and a steady tread in cellos and double basses, woodwind and violas play the long and broad melody in A flat, *andante*, nobilmente e semplice, which is to haunt the whole Symphony like a presence:

Ex. 24

One cannot call it a motto-theme, but it is an *idée fixe*, and after its first quiet statement, the full orchestra repeat it fortissimo. It gently subsides back to woodwind and violas and abruptly switches to D minor, an extraordinary choice of key for the first *allegro* of a Symphony in A flat.* The *idée fixe* has been a 50-bar prelude to a movement that is probably Elgar's finest symphonic structure and one that never for a moment deserves any adjective such as complacent or comfortable, for the music is constantly disturbed, restless and volatile in mood. A change from 2/2 to 6/4 brings a slackening of impulse and an expressive new theme for strings:

Ex. 25

The second subject

Ex. 26

is hardly established before the tumultuousness returns, the music striding and leaping along in fifths, with characteristic brass fanfares, the whole passage culminating in the emphatic statement (horn parts marked tutta forza) of *x* in Ex. 26. Elgar has been criticised for his seemingly insensitive inflation and coarsening of some of his tender themes – examples occur in the *Introduction and Allegro*, the Second Symphony, and especially in the Violin Concerto where the wistful 'Windflower' theme in the first

* Sir Adrian Boult was told that this juxtaposition of keys resulted from a bet placed with Elgar that he could not compose a symphony in two keys at once.

movement is at one point blared out savagely – but in this particular case the phrase seems strong enough to withstand its
grandiose metamorphosis.

The grandeur gives way to the first return of the prelude-theme
(Ex. 24), almost tentative and hesitant now on muted horns, and
soon to be swept aside by another animated episode of swiftly
altering tonality which develops the *allegro* material until it
becomes grandioso and eighteen bars later again changes character,
by way of a ritardando, to a mysterious passage which, Elgar
specified, 'should be played in a veiled and remote manner'. Harps,
solo violin, solo cello, and woodwind create this atmosphere, the
prelude-theme is hinted at, its calming influence again rejected
in favour of a restless agitation which alternates with a caressing
development of second-subject material. But the fiercer element
persists in the recapitulation, driving to a climax. Then (*poco meno
mosso*) gradually spreading from the last desks of the violins and
violas, the great tune of Ex. 24 struggles through to affirmation
by the brass, but the end of the coda is again 'veiled'. The final
pages of this movement are a *locus classicus* for Elgar's mastery of
the orchestra, producing an effect of magical stillness with econo-
mical means but a wealth of detail and instruction: strings ponticello, harp arpeggios, muted horns and strings, a clarinet solo
and solo double bass. There is the same certainty of achievement
in this movement as in the *Enigma Variations*: the scoring is
mature and, big though the canvas is, the close relationship of all
the material ensures that the music's logic is always apparent.

From the second movement, *allegro molto* and chiefly in F sharp
minor, Elgar withheld the title of scherzo, with its implications of
humour and jesting. Again the mood is restless, short phrases
scurrying about and rhythmic figures leaping in woodwind and
strings. The second subject is march-like in character but is never
given a chance to settle into a broad tune. A middle section in
B flat major is yet another evocation of childhood memories,
airily and delicately scored for strings and woodwind. It was this
enchanting episode that Elgar asked orchestras to play 'like
something you hear down by the river'. It recurs, the solo violin
passage now slightly more elaborate, and merges into the march-
tune which gradually slows down over an insistent and still
slightly sinister rhythm provided by harps, timpani, side-drum

and tambourine until the strings are left, sustained only by a chord on bassoons. The violins' and violas' F sharp veers into D major for the opening of the *adagio*, of which the beautiful main theme is note for note that of the second movement's impulsive main theme now becalmed into a melody of limitless consolatory powers:

Ex. 27

This justly extolled and mellow movement is unique among Elgar slow movements in the absence of that anguished yearning quality usually to be found in his quieter passages. There is no *Angst* here, instead a benedictory tranquillity which is marvellously sustained and intensified when the second subject arrives and still more so at cue 104 when a third tune, new and yet seeming to sum up the previous two themes, is introduced by the strings, molto espressivo e sostenuto. The effect of this new melody is as striking as that of the Angel's Farewell in *The Dream of Gerontius*. Like that great tune, it guides the music to a hushed and serene close, the last two notes being breathed by a solo clarinet as a postlude to the triplets on the muted brass. Elgar seems, for once, to have been at peace within himself.

The finale begins in D minor, *lento,* with an introduction which includes adumbrations of one of the chief themes of the movement (a march-rhythm once again) and fragments of Ex. 24, as well as another theme from the first movement. When the music plunges into the *allegro* we can hear that the restlessness of the first two movements has not been banished by the *adagio*. Two strong themes – the second of which has been quoted in Ex. 2 – are succeeded by the impulsive march-rhythm which swaggers its way to a climax marred by a too facile reliance on sequences and stilled by the ghostly return of Ex. 24 in E flat minor. This echo of the past engenders transformation of the march-rhythm, by a lengthening of its notes, into a splendid aspiring melody, but this mood of high romance has to give way to further development of the earlier themes, sometimes portentously and sometimes with the same air of fantasy that danced from the B flat major section – the 'river music' – of the second movement. Elgar is preparing for the inevitable climax of the Symphony, the triumphant return of the opening melody, Ex. 24. It returns grandioso (poco largamente), orchestrated with glittering splendour. But its processional way is not unmarred by memories of the struggles that have gone before: the flow of the theme is broken up by irregular 'crashes' and flourishes from strings and woodwind.

SYMPHONY NO. 2 IN E FLAT MAJOR, OP. 63

The essence of the Second Symphony is contained in the lines from Shelley's *Invocation* which precede the printed score but in the manuscript were written at the end:

> Rarely, rarely comest thou,
> Spirit of Delight!

This is one clue to the emotional programme of the Symphony. Others are in the names Venice and Tintagel, written at the end of the score, and in more lines of Shelley quoted by Elgar to Lady Colvin while he was composing it:

> I do but hide
> Under these notes, like embers, every spark
> Of that which has consumed me.

Clearly, then, Elgar was implying that this Symphony represented a powerful personal and spiritual experience of some kind. Coming so soon after the Violin Concerto and preceding *The Music Makers* it represents part of a trilogy of which Elgar himself said (to Alice Stuart-Wortley): 'I have written out my soul in the concerto,

Sym. II and the Ode and you know it . . . in these three works I have *shewn* myself.'

Perhaps to divert public attention from the intimate personal character of the music, he dedicated it to the memory of King Edward VII and it was assumed that the *larghetto*, in the character of a funeral march, was an elegy for the dead monarch. In fact, as already pointed out, some of the movement was sketched in 1904 shortly after the sudden death of his Liverpool friend Alfred Rodewald, an event that shattered Elgar. No doubt as the music matured it acquired other associations, but to hear in it only a loyal lament for the demise of Edwardian splendour is to misinterpret an autobiographical document which reflects the nature of its creator in all its complexity and contradictions. It is interesting to notice that an anonymous critic who attended one of its early performances detected 'pessimism and rebellion'.

In the autumn of 1909 Elgar began to look through the sketches of the Symphony he had contemplated writing in 1903–4, but he was preoccupied with the Violin Concerto. After a motor tour of Cornwall in April 1910, during which he visited Alice Stuart-Wortley at Tintagel, he completed the Concerto and took up the Symphony again in October when he said that he was 'weaving strange and wonderful memories into very poor music'. He began to assemble his fragments into an organised structure in the first two months of 1911, telling Mrs Stuart-Wortley that he had 'recorded last year [1910] in the first movement . . . I have worked at fever heat and the thing is tremendous in energy'. He completed it on 28 February 1911 and it received its first performance in London on 24 May, less than a month before the coronation of King George V. The audience obviously found it much more difficult to grasp than either the First Symphony or the Violin Concerto, both of which had had rapturous receptions. They were alienated by its quixotic moods, its unexplained and puzzling episodes and its quiet, reflective ending; and, to quote Elgar's description, they 'sat there like stuffed pigs'.

There is never any doubt of the 'tremendous energy' of which Elgar wrote: few symphonies begin so excitingly, with such an impression of bursting exuberance as violins and cellos play their repeated B flats, followed by a characteristic upward swoop of a sixth:

Ex. 28

After eight bars the tempo is quickened as another insistent theme appears, only two bars long, to be followed by two more two-bar themes.

A feature of this Symphony is the shortness of the themes, which are all closely related and capable of lengthy development so that there is no impression of short-windedness. Whereas the *idée fixe* of the First Symphony is a long melody, the motto of the Second, the 'Spirit of Delight' phrase, is epigrammatic (marked *a* in Ex. 28). At bar 27 the tempo slackens, speeds up at 31, slows again at 40, speeds up at 47, and so on throughout the whole kaleidoscopic movement. It is at bar 47 that the first theme of the second-subject group appears, the epitome of Elgarian yearning and unease as is indicated by its restless tonality. The lyrical episode that follows is in Elgar's finest vein of poetic nostalgia, cellos marked dolce e delicato, divided violas and woodwind snatches. The episode is short-lived and the impetuous energy of the opening returns in extra force, sometimes stridently scored for brass and woodwind and with the dolce e delicato theme now brazened forth accompanied by trumpet flourishes.

Soon the passion is spent and a curious, passionately sinister passage ensues, introduced by muted strings, muted horns and eight hollow notes on the harp. Over an extraordinary throbbing of timpani and plucked basses the cellos in their highest register (cue 28) sing a new and expressive melody, a heart-cry for the unattainable if ever there was one. Expressive of what? Elgar gave one clue in a letter to Mrs Stuart-Wortley: 'I have written the *most extraordinary* passage ... a sort of malign influence wandering thro' the summer night in the garden.' It is indeed a sinister nocturne, and its sinister character is banished only by the return of the 'Spirit of Delight' phrase and by a variant of the second subject marked pianissimo, dolcissimo and tranquillo. But the throbbing returns, the violins elaborating what had earlier been background texture.

The eerie vision fades and the movement turns back to the animation of the opening as Elgar makes for the recapitulation of Ex. 28, heralded by ferocious blows on the timpani. During the emphatic triple forte assertion of the 'Spirit of Delight' phrase there is a tiny pause, like a snatched breath, which splits the theme in two after the two upbeat quavers, a dramatic means of ensuring the utmost impact from this re-entry of the main character. The elaborate recapitulation is brilliantly, even too brilliantly, scored – for there is a harshness about the sound that causes the music to glitter rather than to shine. The second-subject group is dwelt on lovingly and again the eight harp notes occur. But this time they are not the prelude to a nightmare but to the 'Spirit of Delight' in consoling mood. Elgar then girds his loins for a final assault and the 'Spirit' is thundered forth to bring the movement to an end in a swirling ascent for the whole orchestra. It is a great movement if the conductor has a sense of its architecture and does not drag the tempo, although it is a little too long and a little too contrived in its contrasts of light and dark. But its almost physical high spirits and the mysterious enigma of its tragic central episode are manifestations of a genius at work with an orchestra.

The *larghetto* in C minor is as noble a movement as any in the symphonic range. Its compassionate seven bars of introduction establish a thematic link with bars 9–10 of the first movement. The main theme, a march-like melody of simple grandeur, is sepulchrally scored – three flutes, clarinets and bass clarinet, trumpet and trombone and first violins play the melody over the solemn tread of bassoons, horns, tuba, timpani, harps and strings. There are three other themes: a lament in thirds for oboe, cor anglais and clarinet, a gently compassionate one for strings, made memorable by the violas' melisma in the fourth bar

Ex. 29

and a proud expression of grief, nobilmente e semplice, for horns and cellos.

With immense sureness of aim, Elgar gradually screws up the tension of this movement towards its central episode when the march returns, leaden-footed with grief, and oboe and cor anglais begin a lament from which the oboe detaches itself mezzoforte – though still accompanied pianissimo by the cor anglais – to weave a counterpoint (molto rubato quasi ad lib.) above the tread of the brass and basses and the washes of tone from the divided strings. A further impassioned climax is reached before, in the closing pages, the 'Spirit of Delight' theme alights like some ministering angel, first on clarinets, then violas and violins; the music of the introduction returns, and the trombones utter a violent shudder before the gentle close. It is Elgar's remarkable achievement to have composed, in this movement, music to which his countrymen automatically now turn for an expression of national mourning but which is really a deeply personal emanation of sorrow, stemming originally from that black day in November 1903 when Rodewald died and Elgar gave way to his despair: 'I broke down and went out, and it was night to me . . . I am utterly broken up.'

The rondo third movement again raises in acute form the question of the Symphony's descriptive basis because it contains a passage that must have had a programmatic origin. Elgar attached a literary association to it and there are other reliably documented accounts of 'explanations' for it. The opening theme reverts to the restless, energetic mood of the first movement and is first introduced divided between woodwind and strings, a finely scored episode, although the music is rhythmically alert – much use being made of the figure ♫♩ – it is only superficially gay. Beneath the exuberant surface foreboding lurks, and even the grand striding second subject in C minor gives no security of atmosphere.

Woodwind introduce a quieter, more pastoral theme before the main rondo returns as a soft rhythmical counterpoint to the new tune. Out of their conflict grows the astonishing episode when, over an E flat pulsing, the 'malign influence' theme for cellos in the first movement returns (cue 119), its character now aggressive and insistent. Drums throb and beat, brass roar out the dominating rhythmic figure like some malevolent hammering and after a tremendous cymbal crash a diminuendo begins and the frightening vision fades as though it had never been. There is a shortened recapitulation of the C minor theme and a coda of exceptional vivacity and excitement, full of cross-rhythms and orchestral virtuosity.

What does that violent interruption signify? When he sketched some of this Symphony in Venice in 1910 Elgar thought of the *larghetto* and rondo as representations of the contrast between the inside of St Mark's and the bustle of the Piazza, but does not seem to have pursued the idea very far. He told his friend Canon W. H. T. Gairdner that he compared the passage in its emotional significance to some lines from Tennyson's *Maud* (V, 1):

> Dead, long dead,
> Long dead!
> And my heart is a handful of dust
> And the wheels go over my head,
> And my bones are shaken with pain,
> For into a shallow grave they are thrust,
> Only a yard beneath the street,
> And the hoofs of the horses beat, beat,
> The hoofs of the horses beat,
> Beat into my scalp and brain
> With never an end to the stream of passing feet . . .

The whole passage speaks of sudden death, of no peace beyond the grave. Was its musical equivalent Elgar's recollection of the shock and agony that Rodewald's death produced in him? Was he recalling a visit to Rome in 1909 when police fired on demonstrators during a strike and he 'saw the poor human stains on the stones and the bullet marks on the walls'? Agreeing with Canon Gairdner that the whole Symphony represented the 'passionate pilgrimage' of a soul, he volunteered the information that this third-movement episode represented 'the madness that attends the excess or abuse of passion'. Which can be taken many ways, depending which kind of passion is meant.

The finale, in 3/4 time and E flat, begins as if all frenzy, all restlessness, had gone. The splendid, dignified opening theme holds no memories of what has preceded it, but a subsidiary theme is much jumpier, containing intervals of a fifth, a sixth and an octave and the Elgar fingerprint of a tenuto note. (Has any composer used tenuto more often?) A third nobilmente theme (cue 142), written several years earlier and annotated by Elgar as 'Hans [Richter] himself', restores the air of sober confidence, but for development Elgar plunges into fugal devices, brass fanfares, shrilling woodwind – all the apparatus of restless, fidgety music. This *poco animato* section is often conducted too fast, which has the effect of emphasising the weakness of invention and the incessant repetition of sequences as a mannerism.

The main theme returns and the Symphony seems to be striding towards a triumphant conventional ending when a long diminuendo begins and the 'Spirit of Delight', now very slow and expanded, returns on flutes, clarinets and bassoons, consoling and unattainable, like a great symphonic sigh. The harps' glissandi lend that very Elgarian effect of the music's taking wings, while the whole orchestra caresses the motto-theme. The finale's main theme is heard on the cellos and the work comes to a solemn end, the last four bars being a decrescendo from fortissimo to pianissimo. Whatever or whoever the 'Spirit of Delight' was, it eluded Elgar as it eluded Shelley:

> Thou art Love and Life! Oh, come,
> Make once more my heart thy home.

What Elgar's symphonies mean to English music can be simply stated: they are the first works in this form by an Englishman to retain their place in the orchestral repertoire year after year. They could be played in the company of Beethoven and Brahms and not sound out of place or outfaced. They encouraged the next generation of English composers to reject the idea that the symphony was dead. Vaughan Williams, who had vowed he would not write an orchestral symphony and had spent from 1903–9 working on a choral work in symphonic form, in 1912 began work on his *London Symphony*, which is clearly influenced by Elgar in form and context, and wrote seven more symphonies in the ensuing 45 years. Bax, Bliss, Walton and Rubbra all wrote symphonies.

In 1933, when he was 75, Elgar began work on a Third Symphony, to be Op. 88, commissioned by the BBC at the bidding of Bernard Shaw. He worked in his usual way, producing disconnected fragments of four movements, an *allegro*, *molto maestoso*, an *allegretto*, an *adagio* and a finale, but later in the year the sciatic pain of which he had complained for some time was diagnosed as an incurable cancer. He wrote no more and died on 23 February 1934, after pleading that no one should 'tinker' with the symphony. Sending a theme from the *adagio* to Ernest Newman he wrote: 'Here is my stately sorrow. Naturally what follows brings hope.' Still, then, the 'massive hope for the future' despite the elusiveness of the 'Spirit of Delight'. The sketches* show vitality and harmonic interest. Whether the fallow years since 1920 were over and a genuine new creative spell was beginning must forever remain only a matter for speculation.

* First described by W. H. Reed and published in facsimile in *The Listener*, 28 August 1935, and reprinted in his *Elgar as I Knew Him* (Gollancz, 1936).